Cookie Dough Secrets

1 Basic Cookie Dough

70 Cookie Recipes

♥

Lia Roessner Wilson

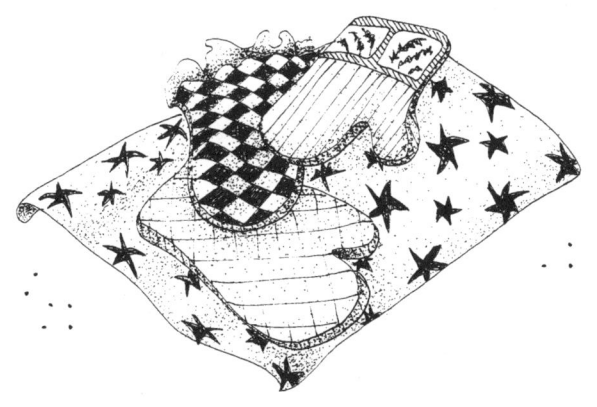

Cookie Dough Secrets
1 Dough
70 Recipes

1st Printing   May 2002

Copyright © 2002
By Cookbook Resources, LLC, Highland Village, Texas. All rights reserved.

ISBN 1-931294-27-5
Library of Congress Number 2002103903

All Rights Reserved. No part of this book may be reproduced in any form without written permission from the publisher, except for brief passages included in a review appearing in a newspaper or magazine.

Front Cover and Illustrations by Nancy Murphy Griffith
Art Direction by Liz Toftness Reinken

Designed and Manufactured in the
United States of America by
Cookbook Resources LLC
541 Doubletree Drive
Highland Village, Texas 75077
Toll free 866-229-2665
www.cookbookresources.com

Preserving
The Family Meal

70 Easy to Make, Distinctive Cookies from One Dough
♥ ♥ ♥

By adding as few as 2 or 3 ingredients to our simple, Basic Cookie Dough, you can create 70 delicious cookies in many shapes and sizes.

Look for this helpful heart because it shows you the really fast and easy recipes.

All these cookie recipes are easy to make. Although it's not necessary, you can make the dough ahead of time and keep it refrigerated until you're ready to bake. Just take it out, warm it up and you're halfway to having fresh, hot cookies. You can even freeze the dough for up to several weeks. Just thaw, bring it to room temperature and you're good to go!

The recipes on the pages that follow give you flexibility in the types of cookies you can make. Don't have a lot of time? Choose one of the drop cookie recipes and whip up a batch in minutes.

Want something a little more out of the ordinary? Pick a pinwheel recipe or a shaped cookie and create a treat that's a little unique.

Looking for something more tasty than store-bought sandwich cookies? Try a jam or creme-filled sandwich cookie recipe. These are just the thing to take to a holiday gathering, serve to the kids as an afternoon snack or give to neighbors as a thoughtful gift.

You'll be amazed at the variety that can be made from one simple dough.

Contents

Introduction 3

Basic Cookie Dough 7

Drop Cookies 8

Shaped Cookies 32

Rolled Cookies 60

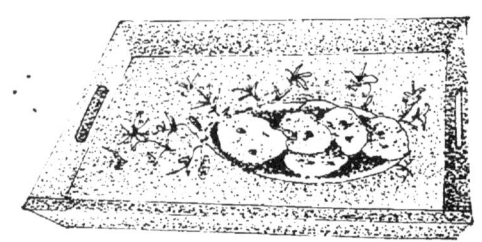

Contents

Pinwheel Cookies 72

Sandwich Cookies 77

Cakes & Bars 85

Index 89

Author Lia Roessner Wilson has a general love of cooking, but is passionate about baking. A member of the IACP (International Association of Culinary Professionals) and a seasoned cook, she creates extraordinary desserts delightful enough for entertaining, yet simple enough for every day. Her first cookbook, Quick Fixes with Mixes, has been showcased several times on QVC.

Lia's most enjoyable role is that of mother to her two sons. She is a mom who believes in making memories for them through the wonderful aromas and treats from her kitchen – the kind of memories that will be treasured for a lifetime.

Basic Cookie Dough

1/2 cup (1 stick) butter or margarine, softened
1 cup sugar
1 egg
1/2 teaspoon vanilla
1/2 teaspoon salt
1 teaspoon baking powder
2 cups flour

In large bowl, cream butter and sugar. Add egg and vanilla and beat until light and fluffy.

In medium bowl, sift salt, baking powder and flour together. Gradually add to butter mixture, beating well after each addition.

Cover and refrigerate dough until ready to use. Warm to room temperature before using unless recipe specifies otherwise.

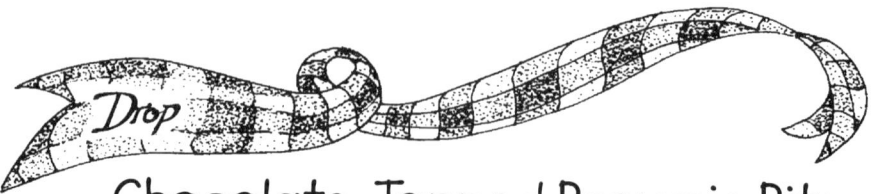

Chocolate-Topped Brownie Bites

Looking and tasting like little bits of brownie, these cookies are fast to make and will disappear even faster.

1 recipe Basic Cookie Dough
4 tablespoons cocoa powder
1/2 cup milk
1/2 cup chopped nuts
1 cup coconut

Preheat oven to 350°. In medium bowl, combine Basic Cookie Dough with cocoa powder and milk. Beat on low speed to blend.

Stir in nuts and coconut.

Drop by rounded teaspoonfuls onto lightly greased cookie sheet. Bake for 10 minutes. Remove from oven and let cookies cool on cookie sheet for 1 minute, then transfer to cooling rack. When cool, spoon about 1 teaspoon chocolate glaze over the top of each cookie. Let chocolate set before serving or storing. (Makes 4 to 4 1/2 dozen.)

Chocolate Glaze

1 cup semi-sweet chocolate chips
6 tablespoons margarine or shortening

Combine chocolate and shortening in small saucepan and melt over very low heat, stirring constantly until mixture is smooth. Remove from heat and use immediately.

Brandied Fruitcake Cookies

A hearty, holiday cookie that's big on fruitcake flavor. These will appeal to those who like fruitcake flavor but aren't crazy about spices. They have a moist texture and their light color lets the colorful fruits and nuts show through.

♥ ♥ ♥

1/2 cup brandy
1 cup fruitcake mix (candied fruit)
1 recipe Basic Cookie Dough
1 tablespoon buttermilk
1 teaspoon orange extract
1 cup chopped pecans
1 cup raisins

In small saucepan, heat brandy almost to boiling. Pour over fruitcake mix and let sit for 20 minutes. Drain and reserve brandy. Set fruit aside.

Preheat oven to 375°. In medium bowl, combine Basic Cookie Dough with reserved brandy, buttermilk and orange extract. Beat until dough is well blended.

Stir in fruit, pecans and raisins.

Drop by heaping teaspoonfuls onto lightly greased cookie sheet. Bake for 10 to 12 minutes or until lightly browned around edges.

Remove from oven and let cookies cool on cookie sheet for 1 minute, then transfer to cooling rack. (Makes 4 to 5 dozen.)

Basic Cookie Dough Recipe on Page 7

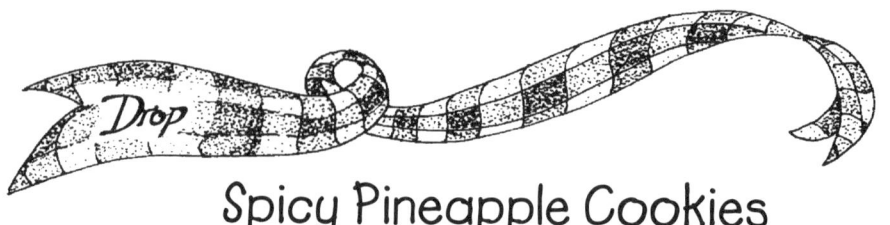

Spicy Pineapple Cookies

1 recipe Basic Cookie Dough
1 teaspoon cinnamon
$1/2$ teaspoon ground nutmeg
$1/4$ teaspoon ground cloves
$2/3$ cup crushed pineapple, very well drained

Preheat oven to 375°. In medium bowl, combine Basic Cookie Dough with cinnamon, nutmeg, cloves and pineapple. Beat until dough is thoroughly blended.

Drop by heaping teaspoonfuls onto ungreased cookie sheet. Bake for 13 to 15 minutes or until edges are lightly browned. Remove from oven and let cookies cool on cookie sheet for 1 minute, then transfer to cooling rack. (Makes 3 $1/2$ to 4 dozen.)

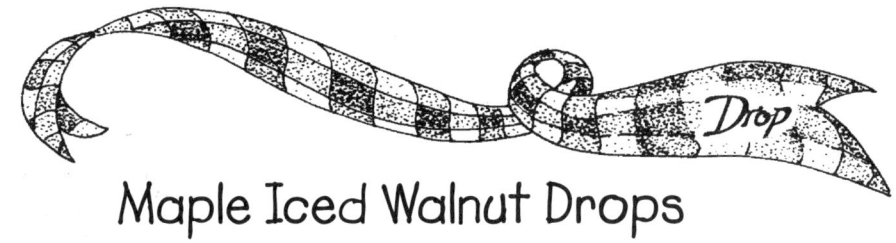

Maple Iced Walnut Drops

Real maple syrup is the key to making these tasty cookies. It gives the icing a strong maple flavor that complements the flavor of the walnuts in the cookies. These take very little time to make, especially if you whip up the icing while the first batch is baking.

1 recipe Basic Cookie Dough
2 cups coarsely chopped walnuts

Preheat oven to 350°. In medium bowl, mix walnuts with Basic Cookie Dough.

Drop by heaping teaspoonfuls onto ungreased cookie sheet. Bake for 10 to 12 minutes or until lightly browned around edges.

Remove from oven and let cookies cool on cookie sheet for 1 minute, then transfer to cooling rack. When cool, frost with maple icing.

Maple Icing

3 tablespoons butter or margarine, softened
1 1/2 cups powdered sugar
1/4 cup maple syrup

Combine butter, powdered sugar and maple syrup in medium bowl. Beat until well blended and mixture is smooth.

Basic Cookie Dough Recipe on Page 7

Mocha Chip Drops

These light cookies have a delicate mocha flavor and are studded with chocolate chips.

    1 teaspoon instant coffee
    2 tablespoons half-and-half or milk
    1 recipe Basic Cookie Dough
    1/2 cup shortening
    1/2 teaspoon almond extract
    1 cup mini-chocolate chips

Preheat oven to 375°. In small bowl, stir coffee into half-and-half to dissolve. Set aside.

In medium bowl, combine Basic Cookie Dough with shortening, almond extract and coffee mixture. Beat until dough is well blended.

Stir in chocolate chips.

Drop by heaping teaspoonfuls onto ungreased cookie sheet. Bake for 10 minutes. Remove from oven and let cookies cool on cookie sheet for 1 minute, then transfer to cooling rack. (Makes 4 to 4 1/2 dozen.)

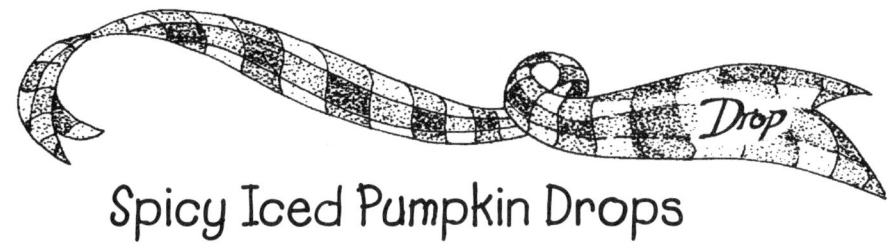

Spicy Iced Pumpkin Drops

One of my favorite recipes, this slightly cake-like cookie has a wonderful flavor and moist texture. One of its best features is that it keeps very well if tightly covered. The flavor just gets better as the cookies sit for a day or so.

1 recipe Basic Cookie Dough
1/2 cup shortening
1 cup canned pumpkin
1/2 teaspoon baking soda
1 teaspoon cinnamon
1/2 teaspoon ground nutmeg
1 cup coarsely chopped walnuts
1 cup raisins

Preheat oven to 350°. In large bowl, combine Basic Cookie Dough with shortening, pumpkin, baking soda, cinnamon and nutmeg. Beat until dough is well blended.

Stir in walnuts and raisins.

Drop by heaping teaspoonfuls onto ungreased cookie sheet. Bake for 15 minutes. Remove from oven and let cookies cool on cookie sheet for 1 minute, then transfer to cooling rack. (Makes 4 to 5 dozen.)

When cool, ice with Orange Frosting.

Orange Frosting

2 cups powdered sugar
1/2 cup butter or margarine, softened
4 tablespoons orange juice

In medium bowl, cream sugar and butter. Beat in orange juice and mix until mixture is smooth. (You may want to add a bit more or less orange juice to get the consistency you want.)

Basic Cookie Dough Recipe on Page 7

White Chocolate Cherry Rounds

1 recipe Basic Cookie Dough
1/4 cup shortening
1/4 cup packed brown sugar
1 tablespoon milk
1 cup white chocolate chips
1 cup chopped maraschino cherries, drained, patted dry

Preheat oven to 375°. In large bowl, combine Basic Cookie Dough with shortening, brown sugar and milk. Beat until well-blended.

Stir in white chocolate chips and cherries.

Drop by heaping teaspoonfuls onto ungreased cookie sheet. Bake for 10 to 12 minutes, just until edges begin to brown.

Remove from oven and let cookies cool on cookie sheet for 1 minute. Transfer to cooling rack. (Makes 3 to 4 dozen.)

Pfeffernuesse

1 recipe Basic Cookie Dough
¼ cup buttermilk
¼ cup molasses
½ teaspoon ginger
½ teaspoon cinnamon
¼ teaspoon ground cloves
¼ teaspoon black pepper

Preheat oven to 350°. In medium bowl, combine Basic Cookie Dough with buttermilk, molasses, ginger, cinnamon, cloves and pepper. Beat until dough is thoroughly blended.

Drop by rounded teaspoonfuls onto lightly greased cookie sheet. Bake for 10 minutes or until edges are lightly browned.

Remove from oven and let cookies cool on cookie sheet for 1 minute, then transfer to cooling rack. (Makes 4 dozen.)

Basic Cookie Dough Recipe on Page 7

Applesauce Drops

A moist, cake-like cookie loaded with texture and the sweet taste of apples. They have a light, delicate flavor.

1 recipe Basic Cookie Dough
½ cup packed brown sugar
1 cup applesauce
2 cups quick-cooking oats
1 cup raisins

Preheat oven to 375°. In medium bowl, combine Basic Cookie Dough with brown sugar, applesauce and oats. Beat until well blended. Stir in raisins.

Drop by rounded teaspoonfuls onto lightly greased cookie sheet.

Bake for 10 to 12 minutes or until lightly browned around edges. Remove from oven and let cookies cool on cookie sheet for 1 minute, then transfer to cooling rack. (Makes 3½ to 4 dozen.)

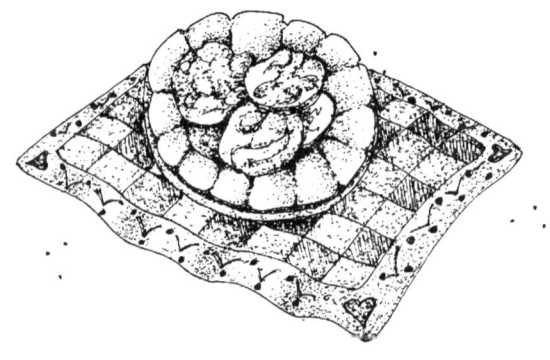

Brandy-Dipped Apricot Delights

1/2 cup brandy
1 cup chopped dried apricots
1 recipe Basic Cookie Dough
1 tablespoon buttermilk

In small saucepan, heat brandy almost to boiling. Pour over apricots and set aside for 20 minutes to soften. Drain and reserve brandy. Set apricots aside.

Preheat oven to 375°. In medium bowl, combine Basic Cookie Dough with buttermilk and reserved brandy. Beat until dough is well-blended. Stir in apricots.

Drop by heaping teaspoonfuls onto lightly greased cookie sheet. Bake for 10 to 12 minutes, just until edges begin to brown.

Remove from oven and let cookies cool on cookie sheet for 1 minute, then transfer to cooling rack. When cool, frost with Brandy Icing. To frost, either dip cookies in the icing, letting excess drip off and then place on wax paper to set. Or, you can put a sheet of wax paper under cooling rack and spoon icing over cookies, letting wax paper catch drips.

Brandy Icing

3 cups powdered sugar
3 tablespoons milk
4-5 tablespoons brandy

In medium bowl, combine powdered sugar with milk and brandy. Beat until icing mixture is smooth. Add additional powdered sugar if icing is too thin or additional brandy if it's too thick.

Basic Cookie Dough Recipe on Page 7

Hearty Carrot Cookies

These scrumptious, cake-like little treats cause very little guilt when I eat more than I should. Loaded with healthy ingredients like carrots, oats and raisins, how can they be anything but good for you?

1 recipe Basic Cookie Dough
½ cup packed brown sugar
1 cup shredded, peeled carrots
1 teaspoon cinnamon
½ teaspoon ground nutmeg
2 cups quick-cooking oats
1 cup raisins
1 cup coarsely chopped walnuts or pecans

Preheat oven to 375°. In large bowl, combine Basic Cookie Dough with brown sugar, carrots, cinnamon and nutmeg. Beat until well blended. Beat in oats. Stir in raisins and nuts.

Drop by heaping teaspoonfuls onto lightly greased cookie sheet and bake for 10 minutes or until lightly browned around edges.

Remove from oven and let cookies cool on cookie sheet for 1 minute, then transfer to cooling rack. (Makes 4 ½ to 5 dozen.)

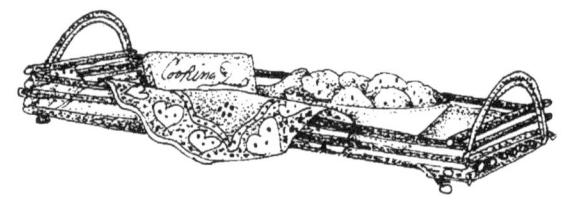

Banana Cookies with Banana Frosting

These cookies are light and crispy with a bold banana flavor! For even better flavor, toast the nuts before adding to the dough by baking on a cookie sheet for 5 minutes at 350°. These also taste great either with or without the frosting.

1 recipe Basic Cookie Dough
1/2 cup shortening
1/2 cup packed brown sugar
3/4 cup mashed ripe bananas
2/3 cup quick-cooking oats
1 cup chopped nuts (optional)

Preheat oven to 350°. In large bowl, combine Basic Cookie Dough with shortening, brown sugar and bananas and mix thoroughly. Blend in oats. Stir in nuts (if you want).

Drop by heaping teaspoonfuls onto ungreased cookie sheet and bake for 15 minutes, or until edges are lightly browned.

Remove from oven and let cookies cool on cookie sheet for 1 minute, then transfer to cooling rack. (Makes 4 1/2 to 5 dozen.)

When cool, ice with Banana Frosting.

Banana Frosting

2 tablespoons butter or margarine, softened
1/4 cup mashed ripe bananas
1 teaspoon lemon juice
2 cups powdered sugar

In medium bowl, cream butter, bananas and lemon juice until smooth. Add powdered sugar one cup at a time blending well after each addition. Beat until smooth.

Basic Cookie Dough Recipe on Page 7

Drop

Date-Studded Orange Cookies

Another winning flavor combination, dates, orange and cinnamon go together like they were made for each other. They're all in this easy to make, but fabulous, cookie. If dates aren't handy, or aren't your preference, substitute raisins instead. You'll get the same great flavor.

    1 recipe Basic Cookie Dough
    1/2 cup shortening
    1/2 cup packed brown sugar
    1/2 teaspoon baking soda
    1 teaspoon cinnamon
    2 tablespoons orange zest
    1 egg white
    1 cup chopped dates
    1/2 cup coconut

Preheat oven to 375°. In large bowl, combine shortening, brown sugar, baking soda, cinnamon, orange zest and egg white with Basic Cookie Dough. Beat until well blended.

Stir in dates and coconut.

Drop by heaping teaspoonfuls onto ungreased cookie sheet. Bake for 10 to 12 minutes or until nicely browned.

Remove from oven and let cookies cool on cookie sheet for 1 minute before transferring to cooling rack. (Makes 4 to 4 1/2 dozen.)

Crispy Pecan Thins

These thin little cookies are crisp and crunchy. If you like the taste of cinnamon, add half a teaspoonful to the dough along with the other ingredients.

    1 recipe Basic Cookie Dough
    1/2 cup shortening
    3/4 cup packed brown sugar
    1/2 teaspoon baking soda
    1 egg white
    1 1/2 cups coarsely chopped pecans

Preheat oven to 375°. In large bowl, combine shortening, brown sugar, baking soda and egg white with Basic Cookie Dough. Beat until well blended.

Stir in pecans.

Drop by heaping teaspoonfuls onto ungreased cookie sheet. Bake for 12 to 14 minutes or until nicely browned all over.

Remove from oven and let cookies cool on cookie sheet for 1 minute before transferring to cooling rack. (Makes 4 to 4 1/2 dozen.)

Basic Cookie Dough Recipe on Page 7

Oatmeal Raisin Cookies

1 recipe Basic Cookie Dough
1/2 cup shortening
1/2 cup packed brown sugar
1/2 teaspoon baking soda
1 egg white
3/4 cup quick-cooking oats
3/4 cup raisins

Preheat oven to 375°. In large bowl, combine shortening, brown sugar, baking soda and egg white with Basic Cookie Dough. Beat until well blended.

Stir in oats and raisins.

Drop by heaping teaspoonfuls onto ungreased cookie sheet. Bake for 10 to 12 minutes or until nicely browned.

Remove from oven and let cookies cool on cookie sheet for 1 minute before transferring to cooling rack. (Makes 4 to 4 1/2 dozen.)

Hearty Trail Mix Cookies

There are several varieties of trail mix. I like to find one with colorful chocolate candies, nuts and raisins, but you can use any that appeal to you. You can even make your own if you want. Simply mix together a variety of nuts, chocolate candy or chocolate chips, raisins or other dried fruit in equal proportions.

1 recipe Basic Cookie Dough
$1/2$ cup shortening
$1/2$ cup packed brown sugar
$1/2$ teaspoon baking soda
1 egg white
1 $1/2$ cups trail mix
$3/4$ cup coconut

Preheat oven to 375°. In large bowl, combine shortening, brown sugar, baking soda and egg white with Basic Cookie Dough. Beat until well blended.

Stir in trail mix and coconut.

Drop by heaping teaspoonfuls onto ungreased cookie sheet. Bake for 10 to 12 minutes or until nicely browned.

Remove from oven and let cookies cool on cookie sheet for 1 minute before transferring to cooling rack. (Makes 4 to 4 $1/2$ dozen.)

Basic Cookie Dough Recipe on Page 7

Apple Cranberry Cookies

Apples and cranberries are a wonderful combination and seem especially suited to the Thanksgiving and Christmas holidays. These chunky cookies pack a lot of punch in a small treat. With their spicy flavor and attractive red and white colors, these cookies are great during the holiday season. Try adding a cup of white chocolate chips for a little variety.

1 recipe Basic Cookie Dough
1/2 cup shortening
1/2 cup packed brown sugar
1/2 teaspoon baking soda
1 egg white
1/4 teaspoon ground nutmeg
1/2 teaspoon cinnamon
1/4 teaspoon lemon extract
3/4 cup coarsely chopped walnuts
3/4 cup dried, sweetened cranberries
3/4 cup chopped dried apples

Preheat oven to 375°. In large bowl, combine shortening, brown sugar, baking soda, egg white, nutmeg, cinnamon and lemon extract with Basic Cookie Dough and beat until well blended.

Stir in walnuts, cranberries and dried apples.

Drop by heaping teaspoonfuls onto lightly greased cookie sheet. Bake for 10 to 12 minutes or until nicely browned.

Remove from oven and let cookies cool on cookie sheet for 1 minute before transferring to cooling rack. (Makes 4 to 4 1/2 dozen.)

Ranger Cookies

1 recipe Basic Cookie Dough
½ cup shortening
1 cup packed brown sugar
1 egg
1 teaspoon baking soda
3 cups crisped rice cereal

Preheat oven to 350°. In large bowl, combine Basic Cookie Dough with shortening, brown sugar, egg and baking soda. Beat until well mixed.

Stir in crisped rice.

Drop by heaping teaspoonfuls onto ungreased cookie sheet.

Bake for 10 to 12 minutes or until edges are lightly browned. Remove from oven and let cookies cool on cookie sheet for 1 minute before transferring to cooling rack. (Makes 4 to 4 ½ dozen.)

Basic Cookie Dough Recipe on Page 7

Lemon Zucchini Cookies

Anyone who likes zucchini bread will like the taste of these. Nutty and cake like, these cookies are light in flavor and texture. The slight citrus flavor goes really well with the zucchini.

1 recipe Basic Cookie Dough
$1/2$ cup shortening
$1/2$ teaspoon lemon extract
1 cup grated, unpeeled zucchini
1 cup coconut
$3/4$ cup chopped walnuts

Preheat oven to 375°. In large bowl, combine shortening with Basic Cookie Dough and blend well. Beat in lemon extract, zucchini and coconut. Stir in walnuts.

Drop by heaping teaspoonfuls onto ungreased cookie sheet.

Bake for 15 to 17 minutes or until edges are lightly browned. Remove from oven and let cookies cool on cookie sheet for 1 minute, then transfer to cooling rack. (Makes 6 to 7 dozen.)

Orange Mocha Drops

One of my favorite flavor combinations, chocolate and orange, is combined in this soft, dense cookie. The chocolate cookie has a hint of coffee flavor and the orange icing is tangy and sweet. This is a great cookie for Halloween, with the dark chocolate of the cookie topped by the orange-colored icing.

1 recipe Basic Cookie Dough
$2/3$ cup sour cream
2 teaspoons instant coffee powder
$1/2$ cup hot water
3 (1 ounce) squares unsweetened chocolate, melted

Preheat oven to 375°. In large bowl, beat Basic Cookie Dough with sour cream. Dissolve coffee in hot water and add to dough mixture, blending well. Beat in melted chocolate.

Drop by rounded teaspoonfuls onto ungreased cookie sheet. Bake for 7 minutes. Immediately after removing from oven, transfer cookies to cooling rack. When cool, frost with Orange Icing. (Makes 4 to 4 $1/2$ dozen.)

Orange Icing

2 tablespoons butter or margarine, melted
2 cups powdered sugar
2 tablespoons milk
1 tablespoon orange zest (grated orange rind)

Combine butter, powdered sugar and milk in small bowl. Beat until mixture is smooth. Stir in orange zest.

Basic Cookie Dough Recipe on Page 7

Orange Glazed Fruitcake Rounds

These spicy cookies are crispy on the edges, but soft on the inside and just bursting with fruitcake flavor. The orange glaze really tops them off and looks really pretty against the dark cookie.

1 recipe Basic Cookie Dough
$1/2$ cup shortening
$1/2$ cup molasses
$1/2$ teaspoon cinnamon
$1/4$ teaspoon ground nutmeg
$1/4$ teaspoon ginger
$1/4$ teaspoon cloves
$1/2$ cup quick-cooking oats
1 cup fruitcake mix (soaked in hot water, well drained & dried)*
1 cup coarsely chopped walnuts (optional)

Preheat oven to 350°. In large bowl, combine Basic Cookie Dough with shortening, molasses, cinnamon, nutmeg, ginger and cloves. Beat until well mixed.

Blend in oats and fruitcake mix (and walnuts, if you want).

Drop by rounded teaspoonful onto ungreased cookie sheet. Bake for 13 to 15 minutes. Remove from oven and let cookies cool on cookie sheet for 1 minute, then transfer to cooling rack.

When cool, drizzle Orange Glaze over cookies in a zigzag motion. To do this, I like to use a small sandwich bag with the corner snipped off. I fill the bag, twist the top above the icing, and then snip a tiny piece off the corner. By gently squeezing the bag, twisting it as necessary to keep pressure on the glaze inside, I can get a neat, steady stream of glaze over the cookies.

Orange Glaze

1 1/2 cups powdered sugar
2 tablespoons orange juice
2 teaspoons orange zest (grated orange rind)

Combine powdered sugar and orange juice in small bowl and beat until mixture is smooth. Stir in orange zest.

*To re-hydrate the fruitcake mix so it's softer in the cookies, I pour boiling water over the mix and let it sit for 20 minutes. Then I drain the water off and dry the mix as much as possible with paper towels.

Basic Cookie Dough Recipe on Page 7

White Chocolate Macadamia Nut Cookies

1 recipe Basic Cookie Dough
1/2 cup shortening
1/2 cup packed brown sugar
1/2 teaspoon baking soda
1 egg white
2 cups white chocolate chips
1 cup coarsely chopped macadamia nuts, toasted

Preheat oven to 375°. In large bowl, combine shortening, brown sugar, baking soda and egg white with Basic Cookie Dough. Beat until well blended.

Stir in white chocolate chips and macadamia nuts.

Drop by heaping teaspoonfuls onto ungreased cookie sheet. Bake for 10 to 12 minutes or until nicely browned.

Remove from oven and let cookies cool on cookie sheet for 1 minute before transferring to cooling rack. (Makes 4 to 4 1/2 dozen.)

Traditional Chocolate Chip Cookies

1 recipe Basic Cookie Dough
½ cup shortening
½ cup packed brown sugar
½ teaspoon baking soda
1 egg white
2 cups semi-sweet chocolate chips
1 cup chopped pecans or walnuts

Preheat oven to 375°. In large bowl, combine shortening, brown sugar, baking soda, and egg white with Basic Cookie Dough. Beat until well blended.

Stir in chocolate chips and nuts.

Drop heaping teaspoonfuls onto ungreased cookie sheet. Bake for 10 to 12 minutes or until nicely browned.

Remove from oven and let cookies cool on cookie sheet for 1 minute before transferring to cooling rack. (Makes 4 to 4 ½ dozen.)

Basic Cookie Dough Recipe on Page 7

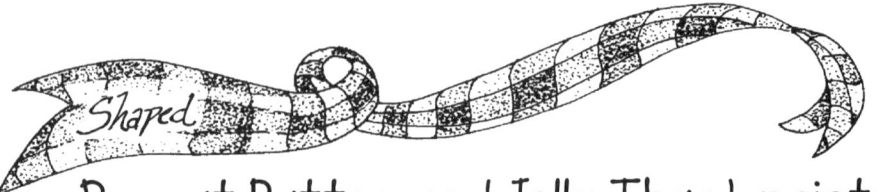

Shaped

Peanut Butter and Jelly Thumbprints

This cookie combines the age-old comfort food favorite peanut butter and jelly, into a delicious cookie that can be made in a snap. Fast and easy!

1 recipe Basic Cookie Dough
1 cup creamy peanut butter
$1/2$ cup packed brown sugar
3 tablespoons sugar
$1/4$ cup grape jam or jelly

Preheat oven to 375°. In large bowl, combine Basic Cookie Dough with peanut butter and brown sugar. Beat until well mixed. (The dough will be very stiff.)

Form dough into balls 1 $1/2$-inch wide. Roll dough balls in sugar and place 2 inches apart on ungreased cookie sheet. Using the back of a blunt handled spoon or your thumb, make an indentation in the top of each ball.

Fill with about $1/2$ teaspoon or less of jelly or jam.

Bake for 8 to 10 minutes, just until edges begin to brown, and remove from oven. Let cookies cool for 1 minute on cookie sheet and then transfer to cooling rack. (Makes 3 $1/2$ to 4 dozen.)

Renna's Cappuccino Drops

What a fun, delicious variation on the peanut butter and chocolate kiss theme! My cousin Renna suggested the combination of coffee, chocolate and white chocolate, and what a hit. The round chocolate cookies look fantastic with the white chocolate kiss sitting on top and they taste great too--just like a smooth cappuccino!

- 1 recipe Basic Cookie Dough
- 2 tablespoons shortening
- 2 tablespoons unsweetened chocolate, melted
- 2 tablespoons instant coffee powder
- 2 tablespoons sugar
- 36-42 white chocolate kisses candies

Preheat oven to 375°. In large bowl, combine shortening, chocolate and coffee powder with Basic Cookie Dough. Mix until well blended and dough is evenly colored.

Place sugar in a shallow dish or bowl.

Form dough into balls 1 1/2 inches in diameter. Roll in sugar to coat, then place 2 inches apart on ungreased cookie sheet. Using your thumb, make a slight indentation in center of each dough ball.

Bake for 5 minutes. Remove from oven and immediately place a candy kiss in the indentation of each cookie, gently pressing down.

Place back in the oven and bake for another 2 minutes. Remove from oven and let cookies cool on cookie sheet for 1 minute, then transfer to cooling rack. (Makes 3 to 3 1/2 dozen.)

Basic Cookie Dough Recipe on Page 7

Chocolate Covered Cherry Delights

What a rich, delicious cookie that's more like candy. The chocolate forms a nice candy-like coating over the dense chocolate cookie. They stay really moist if kept tightly covered.

1 recipe Basic Cookie Dough
2 (1 ounce) squares unsweetened chocolate, melted
36 to 42 maraschino cherries, well drained
    (about one 16-ounce jar)
1 cup semi-sweet chocolate chips
1/2 cup sweetened condensed milk
1 tablespoon maraschino cherry juice

Preheat oven to 350°. In medium bowl, combine melted chocolate with Basic Cookie Dough and beat until well-blended.

Roll pieces of dough into balls about 1 1/2 inches in diameter and place 2 inches apart on ungreased cookie sheet. With your thumb or the blunt handle of a spoon, make an indentation in the center of each dough ball.

Place a cherry in the indentation and press down firmly.

In small saucepan, combine chocolate chips, condensed milk and cherry juice. Stir constantly over low heat until chocolate is melted and mixture is smooth.

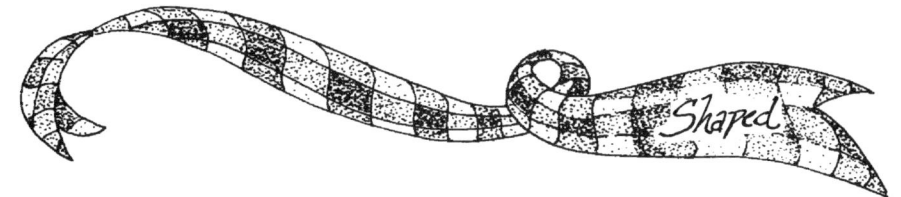

Place a teaspoonful or so of chocolate mixture on top of each cherry and smooth over cookie surface.

Bake for 10 minutes. Remove from oven and let cookies cool on cookie sheet for 1 minute, then transfer to cooling rack. (Makes 3 to 4 dozen.)

To drain the cherries, place them on a paper towel for a few minutes and then pat each one dry before placing it on the cookie.

Basic Cookie Dough Recipe on Page 7

Chocolate Fudge Thumbprints

These are one of my all-time favorites! The fudge filling in the middle is smooth and rich and the chocolate chip cookie base is crispy and delicious. This truly is one of those easy cookies that looks like you spend twice as much time making it as you actually do. Try this when you need an extra-special cookie for an extra-special occasion! (Or just to have at home when you're in the mood for a chocolately treat.)

For a little change in flavor, roll the dough in egg whites to coat, then in 1/2 cup ground hazelnuts instead of the sugar.

1 recipe Basic Cookie Dough
2 tablespoons half-and-half or milk
1/2 cup mini-chocolate chips
2 tablespoons sugar

Preheat oven to 375°. In medium bowl, combine half-and-half with Basic Cookie Dough and beat until blended. Stir in chocolate chips.

Roll dough into balls about 1 1/2 inches wide. Roll balls in sugar to coat and place 2 inches apart on ungreased cookie sheet.

With your thumb or blunt handle of a spoon, make an indentation in the center of each dough ball. Bake for 10 minutes. Remove from oven. If the indentation isn't very apparent, take the back of a spoon and press the center of each cookie to make a small "well."

Make fudge filling and drop about a teaspoonful into each indentation. (Makes 3 1/2 to 4 dozen.)

Fudge Filling

³/₄ cup semi-sweet chocolate chips
1 tablespoon shortening
2 tablespoons corn syrup
1 tablespoon water
1 teaspoon vanilla extract

Combine chocolate chips and shortening in a small saucepan. Cook over very low heat, stirring constantly until chocolate is melted and mixture is smooth.

Remove from heat and stir in corn syrup, water and vanilla.

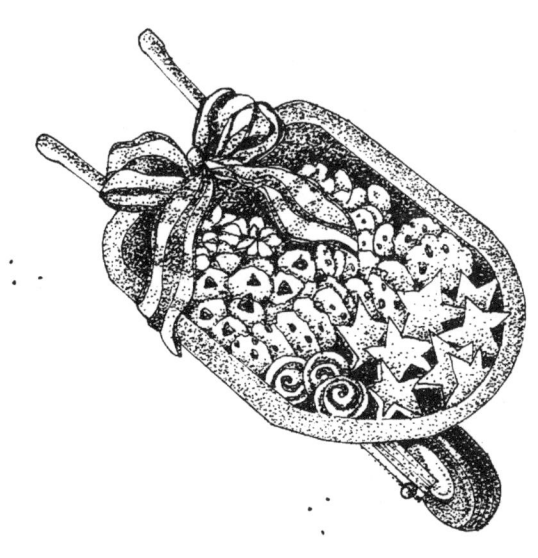

Basic Cookie Dough Recipe on Page 7

Peanut Butter and Chocolate Kisses

Who can resist the flavor of chocolate and peanut butter combined? This cookie is a snap to make and a big favorite. Consider making the dough ahead of time and refrigerating until you're ready to bake the cookies. You'll save loads of time and have a fresh batch of cookies ready in minutes.

♥ ♥ ♥

1 recipe Basic Cookie Dough
1/2 cup peanut butter
3 tablespoons sugar
36-42 chocolate kisses candies

Preheat oven to 375°. In medium bowl combine Basic Cookie Dough with peanut butter. Blend well.

Place sugar in a shallow dish or bowl.

Shape dough into balls 1 1/2 inches in diameter and roll in sugar. Place 2 inches apart on ungreased cookie sheet and using your thumb or rounded handle of a spoon, make a small indentation in the top of each dough ball.

Bake for 5 minutes. Remove from oven and immediately place a chocolate kiss in each indentation, pressing down gently but firmly.

Place back in the oven and bake for another 3 minutes. Remove from oven and let cookies cool on cookie sheet for 1 minute before transferring to cooling rack. (Makes 3 to 3 1/2 dozen.)

Tropical Thumbprint Cookies

These delicious citrus cookies keep very well.

1 recipe Basic Cookie Dough
2 tablespoons lemon zest
1 egg white
1 cup coconut
1/2 cup pineapple jam

Preheat oven to 375°. In medium bowl, add lemon zest to Basic Cookie Dough and beat until well blended. Take heaping teaspoonfuls of dough and roll into 1 1/2-inch balls. Dip each dough ball into egg white, then roll in coconut to coat.

Place 3 inches apart on lightly greased cookie sheet. With rounded, blunt spoon handle or your thumb, make an indentation in center of each dough ball.

Fill with about 1/3 teaspoonful pineapple jam.

Bake for 11 to 13 minutes or until lightly browned. Remove from oven and let cool for 1 minute before transferring to cooling rack. (Makes 3 to 3 1/2 dozen.)

Basic Cookie Dough Recipe on Page 7

Shaped

Chocolate Almond Fingers

Tasty little finger-shaped chocolate cookies loaded with almond flavor, dipped in dark chocolate and rolled in almonds.

1 recipe Basic Cookie Dough
2 (1 ounce) squares unsweetened chocolate, melted
2 tablespoons half-and-half
$1/2$ teaspoon almond extract
1 cup ground almonds

Preheat oven to 375°. In medium bowl, combine Basic Cookie Dough with chocolate, half-and-half and almond extract. Beat until dough is thoroughly mixed.

Using your hands, take small pieces of dough (about a teaspoonful) and roll into "ropes" about 4-inches long and about $1/2$-inch wide. (If dough is sticky or difficult to roll, refrigerate for an hour or two to chill slightly.)

Place 2 inches apart on ungreased cookie sheet. Bake for 10 minutes. Remove from oven and let cookies cool on cookie sheet for 1 minute, then transfer to cooling rack.

When cool, dip half of each cookie in chocolate glaze, then roll glazed portion in almonds. Place on wax paper to set. Once set, cookies can be stored in single layers with wax paper between them. (Makes 3 to $3 \, 1/2$ dozen.)

Chocolate Glaze

1 cup semi-sweet chocolate chips
2 tablespoons shortening

Combine chocolate chips and shortening in small saucepan over low heat. Stir constantly until chocolate is melted and mixture is smooth. Remove from heat.

Chocolate Thumbprints

It may simply be personal preference, but I think these taste especially good with the blackberry jam!

1 recipe Basic Cookie Dough
1/2 teaspoon almond extract
1/2 cup cocoa powder
4 tablespoons milk
1/4 cup sugar
1/4 cup raspberry, cherry or seedless blackberry jam

Preheat oven to 375°. In medium bowl, mix almond extract, cocoa powder and milk with Basic Cookie Dough until completely blended.

Place sugar in shallow bowl.

Take heaping teaspoonfuls of dough and roll into balls about 1 1/2 inches wide. Roll balls in sugar to coat.

Place on lightly greased cookie sheet. With blunt handle of a spoon or your thumb, make an indentation in the top of each dough ball. Fill with 1/3 teaspoon jam.

Bake for 10 minutes. Remove from oven and let cookies cool on cookie sheet for 1 minute before transferring to cooling rack. (Makes 3 to 3 1/2 dozen.)

Basic Cookie Dough Recipe on Page 7

Festive Cranberry Cookies

1 recipe Basic Cookie Dough
1/2 cup shortening
1 tablespoon orange zest (grated orange rind)
2/3 cup chopped dried sweetened cranberries
4 drops red food coloring
1/2 cup finely chopped walnuts or pecans

In medium bowl, blend Basic Cookie Dough with shortening until mixture is smooth. Remove one third of dough and place in small bowl. Add orange zest to this third and beat until well mixed.

Add cranberries and red food coloring to remaining two thirds of dough and beat until dough is evenly colored. Stir in walnuts. Divide dough in half.

Line the bottom of a 9 x 5 (or 8 x 4)-inch loaf pan with plastic wrap or waxed paper. Press half the cranberry dough in the bottom of the loaf pan. Place orange dough evenly on top and press down firmly. Press the remaining half of the cranberry dough evenly over orange dough and press down.

Cover and refrigerate for several hours. When firm, invert pan and peel plastic wrap or waxed paper from dough. Using sharp knife, cut dough into thirds. Slice each third crosswise into 1/4-inch slices and place on ungreased cookie sheet.

Preheat oven to 375°. Bake cookies for 10 minutes or until edges are lightly browned. Remove from oven and let cookies cool on cookie sheet for 1 minute, then transfer to cooling rack. (Makes 3 dozen.)

Peppermint Candy Cane Cookies

These get rave reviews from my 14-year-old, Clayton. "Mom, these are good!" are some of the most satisfying words you'll hear from a teenage son. These red and white cookies shaped like candy canes are very easy to make. If you have the dough ready in the fridge, they take a few minutes to put together and can be a lot of fun for anyone who likes to play with dough.

1 recipe Basic Cookie Dough
1 teaspoon peppermint extract
Several drops red food coloring

Preheat oven to 375°. Mix peppermint extract into Basic Cookie Dough.

Divide dough in half. Color one half red with a few drops of red food coloring.

Take a teaspoonful of red dough and roll into a rope about 6-inches long. Take a teaspoonful of the uncolored dough and roll into a rope the same length. Put the two pieces next to each other, and gently twist. (I generally lift one end and twist toward the middle. I then lift and twist the other end as I place it on the cookie sheet.)

Place on ungreased cookie sheet, shaping the top half of the dough into a crook shape (like a candy cane). Bake for 10 minutes and remove from oven. Let cookies cool on cookie sheet for 1 minute, then transfer to cooling rack. To keep their pretty colors, try not to let them brown too much. (Makes about 1 1/2 to 2 dozen.)

Basic Cookie Dough Recipe on Page 7

Shaped

Chocolate Striped Cookies

These rectangular chocolate cookies have orderly little stripes-- alternating ribbons of chocolate and chocolate-chip flavored dough. They are a big hit at my house. No one can resist chocolate chip cookies and these crisp ones are no exception. They're fun to make too and can be ready at a moment's notice. Simply prepare them ahead of time and refrigerate. You can have fresh, hot cookies in a matter of minutes.

1 recipe Basic Cookie Dough
$1/2$ cup shortening
1 teaspoon rum flavoring
$1/3$ cup chocolate chips, melted
$1/2$ cup chopped nuts
$1/3$ cup miniature chocolate chips

Blend Basic Cookie Dough with shortening until mixture is smooth. Divide dough in half.

Add rum flavoring and melted chocolate to one half and blend well. Stir in nuts. Divide dough in half and set aside.

Add chocolate chips to remaining half and mix well. Divide dough in half.

Line the bottom of a 9 x 5 (or 8 x 4)-inch loaf pan with plastic wrap or waxed paper. Press half of chocolate mixture in the bottom of the loaf pan. Press one half of chocolate chip dough on top and press down firmly.

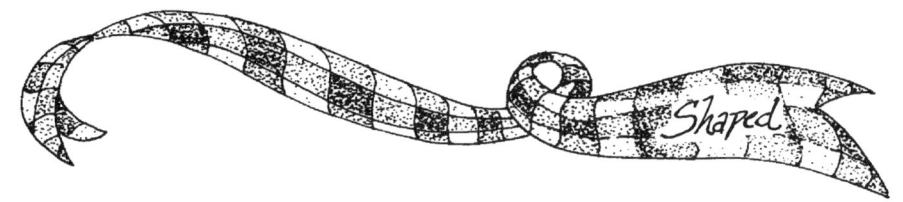

Shaped

Press the remaining half of the chocolate dough on top and press down. Top with remaining chocolate chip dough and press down firmly.

Cover and refrigerate for several hours. When firm, invert pan and peel plastic wrap or waxed paper from dough. Using sharp knife, cut dough into thirds, each piece will be about 3 inches wide. Slice each third crosswise into $1/4$-inch slices and place on ungreased cookie sheet.

Preheat oven to 375°. Bake cookies for 10 minutes or until edges are lightly browned. Remove from oven and let cool on cookie sheet for 1 minute, then transfer to cooling rack. (Makes 3 dozen.)

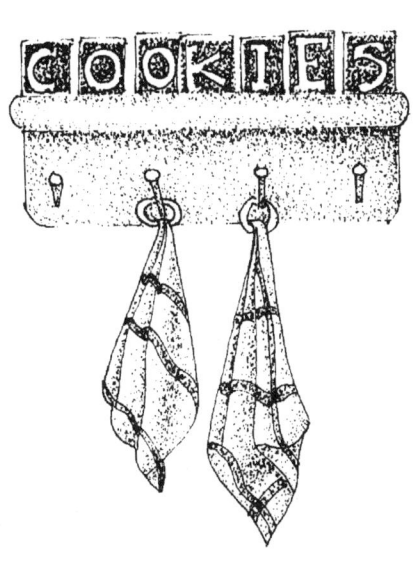

Basic Cookie Dough Recipe on Page 7

Spicy Cinnamon Sugar Twists

1 recipe Basic Cookie Dough
1/4 teaspoon ground nutmeg
2 teaspoons cinnamon, divided
2 pinches ground cloves
1/2 cup sugar

Preheat oven to 375°. In large bowl, add nutmeg, 1 teaspoon cinnamon and cloves to Basic Cookie Dough. Beat until well mixed.

Using your hands, roll heaping tablespoonfuls of dough into ropes 6-inches long. Fold in half and twist two times.

Place on ungreased cookie sheet. Bake for 7 minutes or until edges are lightly browned.

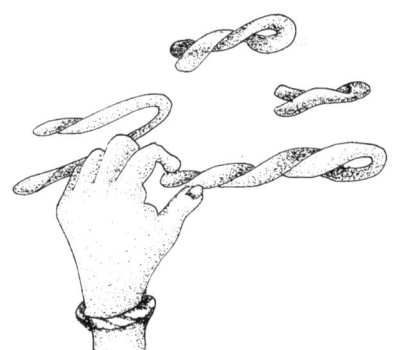

While cookies are baking, combine remaining cinnamon and sugar in small bowl and transfer to shallow dish. Set aside.

Remove cookies from oven and let them remain on cookie sheet for 1 minute, then transfer to cooling rack. When slightly cooled, roll cookies gently in cinnamon and sugar mixture. (Makes 3 to 3 1/2 dozen.)

Heavenly Holiday Rounds

1 recipe Basic Cookie Dough
2 teaspoons rum flavoring
1/8 teaspoon ground nutmeg
2/3 cup finely chopped candied cherries
1/2 cup coconut

In medium bowl, mix rum flavoring and nutmeg into Basic Cookie Dough until thoroughly blended. Stir in cherries.

Divide dough in half. Form each half into a log about 2 inches in diameter. Roll each log in coconut to cover entirely.

Wrap in plastic wrap and refrigerate for several hours.

When ready to bake, set oven temperature to 375°. Cut 1/4-inch slices from each log and place 2 inches apart on ungreased cookie sheet. Bake for 8 to 10 minutes or until very lightly browned around edges. (Makes 3 to 3 1/2 dozen.)

Basic Cookie Dough Recipe on Page 7

Shaped

Chocolate Mint Thins

These crispy, mint-flavored chocolate glazed treats are similar to the Girl Scout cookies so many people know and love!

1 recipe Basic Cookie Dough
2 (1 ounce) squares unsweetened chocolate, melted
2 tablespoons half-and-half
1 teaspoon peppermint extract

In medium bowl, combine Basic Cookie Dough with chocolate, half-and-half and peppermint extract. Beat until dough is thoroughly mixed.

Divide dough in half and roll each half into a log about 2 inches in diameter. Wrap each dough roll carefully in plastic wrap or wax paper and refrigerate for several hours or overnight.

Preheat oven to 375°. Slice each dough roll into pieces $1/8$-inch thick and place 2 inches apart on ungreased cookie sheet. Bake for 7 minutes. Remove from oven and let cookies cool on cookie sheet for 1 minute, then transfer to cooling rack.

When cool, dip each cookie in chocolate coating using fork to lower them into coating and lift them out. Let excess coating drip off. Place on a piece of wax paper to set chocolate coating. Once chocolate is set, cookies can be stored in an airtight container with sheets of wax paper between the layers. (Makes $4 \frac{1}{2}$ to 5 dozen.)

Chocolate Coating

1 (20 ounce) package chocolate coating used for candy-making
6 tablespoons shortening

In small saucepan over very low heat, combine chocolate coating and shortening. Stir constantly until chocolate is melted and mixture is smooth. (Be careful not to cook on medium or higher temperature, because the mixture may harden.) Remove from heat.

Orange Slices

1 recipe Basic Cookie Dough
1 tablespoon orange zest (grated orange rind)
1 teaspoon cinnamon
1/2 cup ground walnuts

In medium bowl, blend beat orange zest and cinnamon into Basic Cookie Dough until well mixed.

Divide dough in half and form each half into a log about 2 inches in diameter.

Roll each log in ground walnuts to cover completely.

Wrap in plastic wrap and refrigerate several hours or until firm.

When ready to bake, preheat oven to 375°. Slice each log into pieces 1/4-inch thick. Place dough slices on ungreased cookie sheet and bake for 8 to 10 minutes or until cookies are lightly browned around edges.

Remove from oven and let cookies cool on cookie sheet for 1 minute before transferring to cooling rack. (Makes 3 to 3 1/2 dozen.)

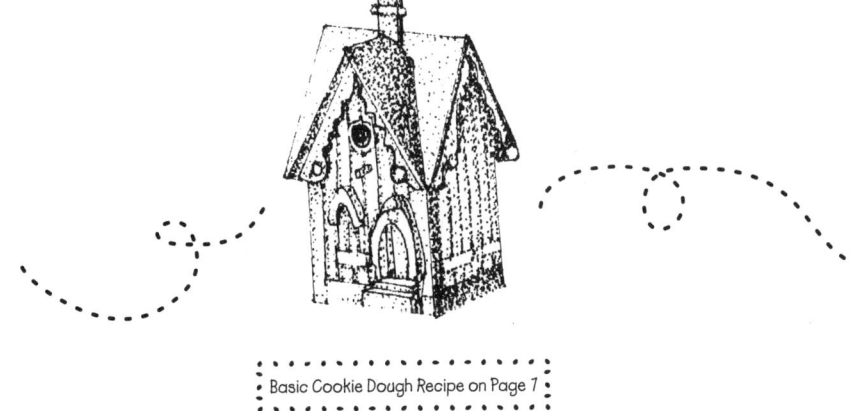

Basic Cookie Dough Recipe on Page 7

Lemon Anise Rounds

1 recipe Basic Cookie Dough
1 teaspoon anise seed
1 teaspoon anise extract
½ teaspoon lemon extract

In medium bowl, mix anise seed, anise extract and lemon extract into Basic Cookie Dough until thoroughly combined.

Divide dough in half. Form each half into a log about 2 inches in diameter. Wrap in plastic wrap and refrigerate for several hours or until firm.

When ready to bake, preheat oven to 375°. Slice each log into pieces ¼-inch thick. Place cookies on ungreased cookie sheet and bake for 10 to 12 minutes or until edges are lightly browned.

Remove from oven and let cookies cool on cookie sheet for 1 minute, then transfer to cooling rack. (Makes 3 to 3 ½ dozen.)

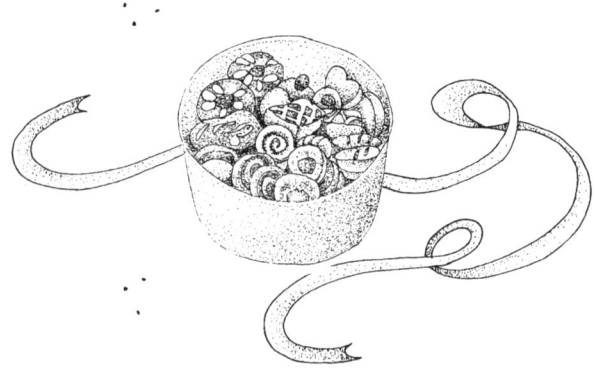

Snappy Peanut Butter Cookies

1 recipe Basic Cookie Dough
1 cup peanut butter, smooth or crunchy
1/4 cup sugar

Preheat oven to 375°. In medium bowl, add peanut butter to Basic Cookie Dough and mix well.

Roll heaping teaspoonfuls of dough into balls and roll in sugar to coat. Place 3 inches apart on ungreased cookie sheet. Make crisscross pattern with fork on top of cookies to flatten.

Bake for 10 minutes. Remove from oven and let cookies cool for 1 minute on cookie sheet before transferring to cooling rack. (Makes 3 to 3 1/2 dozen.)

Basic Cookie Dough Recipe on Page 7

Raisin Gingersnaps

1 recipe Basic Cookie Dough
1 teaspoon baking soda
1/4 cup molasses
1 teaspoon ground ginger
1/4 teaspoon ground cloves
1 cup raisins
1/4 cup sugar

Preheat oven to 375°. In medium bowl, mix baking soda, molasses, ginger and cloves into Basic Cookie Dough until thoroughly blended. Stir in raisins.

Take heaping teaspoonfuls of dough and roll into balls. Roll balls in sugar and place 2 inches apart on lightly greased cookie sheet.

Bake for 10 minutes. Let cookies cool on cookie sheet for 1 minute before transferring to cooling rack. (Makes 3 to 3 1/2 dozen.)

Chocolate-Covered Mocha Balls

Chocolate is so hard to resist. These little cookies look simply delectable. The chocolate coating over these perfectly round, mocha-flavored cookies makes them a star of the dessert table. For a really dramatic effect, top them with silver or gold candy decorations while the coating is still wet.

1 recipe Basic Cookie Dough
4 tablespoons shortening, divided
1 1/2 teaspoons cinnamon
2 tablespoons instant coffee
5 ounces chocolate coating for candy making

Preheat oven to 375°. In large bowl, combine Basic Cookie Dough with 2 tablespoons shortening, cinnamon and instant coffee.

Roll dough into balls 1 1/2 inches in diameter and place 2 inches apart on ungreased cookie sheet.

Bake for 10 minutes, then remove from oven and let cool on cookie sheet for 1 minute. Transfer to cooling rack.

When cool, melt chocolate coating with remaining 2 tablespoons shortening over very low heat, stirring constantly.

Using a fork, lift each cookie ball from underneath (don't skewer them), and then dip in the melted chocolate coating. Place dipped cookies on wax paper until chocolate coating sets, then store in covered container. (Makes 4 to 4 1/2 dozen.)

Basic Cookie Dough Recipe on Page 7

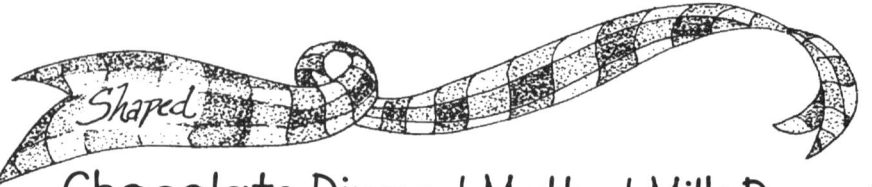

Chocolate Dipped Malted Milk Rounds

These delightful crispy cookies have the flavor of malted milk ball candy. The crunchy cookie is loaded with malted milk flavor and the chocolate coating tops it off. They're easy to make and sharp looking! By shaping the dough into balls, the cookies bake perfectly round. And the chocolate coating over half the cookie looks very stylish.

♥ ♥ ♥

1 recipe Basic Cookie Dough
$1/2$ cup shortening
$1/4$ cup packed brown sugar
1 cup malted milk powder

Preheat oven to 375°. In large bowl, combine Basic Cookie Dough with shortening; blend well. Beat in brown sugar and malted milk powder.

Roll dough into balls 1 $1/2$-inches wide and place 3 inches apart on ungreased cookie sheet. Bake for 10 to 12 minutes until edges are brown.

Remove from oven and let cookies cool on cookie sheet for 1 minute, then transfer to cooling rack.

When cool, dip half of each cookie in chocolate coating, shake excess coating off and place on wax paper to set. (To do this, I find it's easiest to hold the pan with one hand, tilting it so the chocolate pools in the bottom and use my other hand to dip the cookies. I also gently scrape the back of the cookie against the pan's side to remove excess chocolate from the back.)

When chocolate is set, store cookies with a layer of wax paper between them.

Chocolate Coating

10 ounces chocolate-flavored candy coating (like you would use to make almond bark*)
1 tablespoon shortening

In small saucepan, melt chocolate and shortening over very low heat, stirring constantly. When mixture is smooth, remove from heat.

*You can also use 1 1/2 cups milk chocolate chips in place of the chocolate candy coating if you can't locate it. I like the chocolate coating because it sets very quickly and the cookies can be immediately stored.

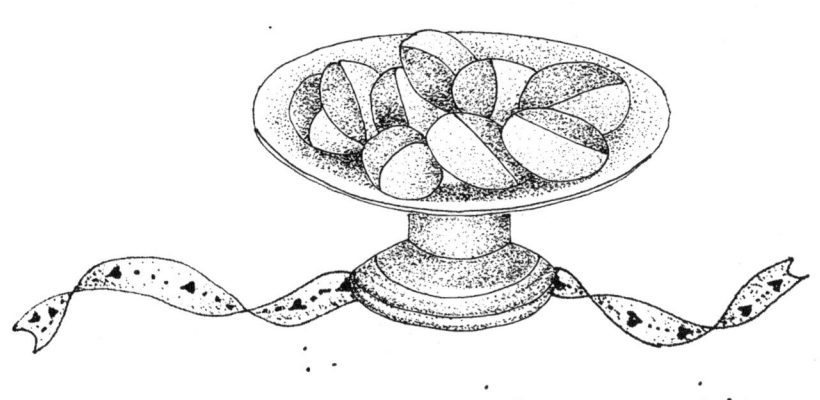

Basic Cookie Dough Recipe on Page 7

Nutty Lemon Rounds

1 recipe Basic Cookie Dough
3 tablespoons lemon juice
2 teaspoons lemon zest (grated lemon rind)
½ cup coconut
½ cup finely chopped pecans
2 tablespoons sugar

Preheat oven to 375°. In medium bowl, combine Basic Cookie Dough with lemon juice and lemon zest. Beat until well blended.

Stir in coconut and pecans.

Roll dough into balls about 1 ½-inches wide and place 2 inches apart on ungreased cookie sheet. Gently flatten with the lightly-greased bottom of a glass dipped in sugar.

Bake for 9 to 11 minutes, just until edges begin to brown. Remove from oven and let cookies cool on cookie sheet for 1 minute, then transfer to cooling rack. (Makes 4 ½ to 5 dozen.)

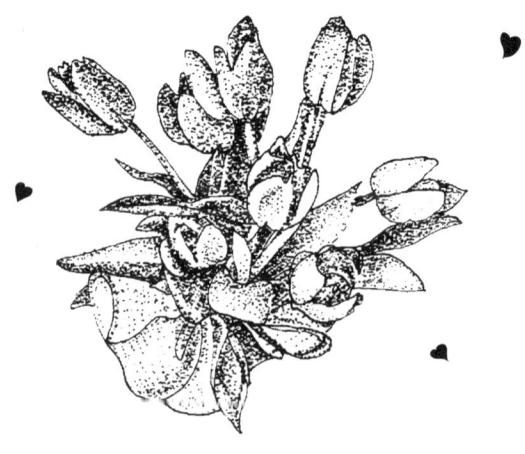

Cherry Caps

What an easy, colorful cookie to lend a holiday touch to your dessert table. For a really festive appearance, make half with green cherries and half with red cherries. If you have the dough made ahead of time, you can make these in minutes and have fresh, warm cookies in a snap.

1 recipe Basic Cookie Dough
1/2 teaspoon almond extract
18-21 candied cherries, halved

Preheat oven to 375°. In medium bowl, combine Basic Cookie Dough with almond extract and beat until thoroughly blended.

Roll pieces of dough into 1-inch balls and place 2 inches apart on ungreased cookie sheet. Top each dough ball with a cherry half, cut side down.

Bake for 10 minutes, then remove from oven and let cookies cool on cookie sheet for 1 minute. Transfer to cooling rack. (Makes 3 to 3 1/2 dozen.)

Basic Cookie Dough Recipe on Page 7

Chocolate Chip Hazelnut Mounds

These light, delicate cookies are loaded with hazelnut flavor and studded with chocolate chips.

    1 recipe Basic Cookie Dough
    1/4 cup shortening
    1 cup mini-chocolate chips
    1 cup ground hazelnuts
    1/4 cup sifted powdered sugar

Preheat oven to 350°. In medium bowl, combine Basic Cookie Dough with shortening and beat until well blended.

Stir in chocolate chips and hazelnuts.

Roll dough into 1-inch balls and place 2 inches apart on ungreased cookie sheet.

Bake for 15 to 18 minutes or until edges just begin to brown. Remove from oven and let cookies cool on cookie sheet for 1 minute, then transfer to cooling rack. When cool, dip cookies in powdered sugar to coat. (Makes 3 1/2 to 4 dozen.)

Molasses Rounds

1 recipe Basic Cookie Dough
1 1/2 teaspoons cinnamon, divided
1 teaspoon ground ginger
1/2 cup molasses
1/2 cup packed brown sugar
2 tablespoons sugar

Preheat oven to 375°. In medium bowl, combine Basic Cookie Dough with 1 teaspoon cinnamon, ginger, molasses and brown sugar. Beat until dough is well blended.

Roll dough into balls about 1 1/2-inches wide. Place 2 inches apart on ungreased cookie sheet.

In small shallow bowl, combine remaining cinnamon and sugar. Stir until well mixed.

Grease bottom of a glass and dip in sugar, then use to flatten each cookie, dipping glass back in the sugar-cinnamon mixture before flattening next cookie.

Bake for 8 to 10 minutes. Remove from oven and let cookies cool on cookie sheet for 1 minute, then transfer to cooling rack. (Makes 4 dozen.)

Basic Cookie Dough Recipe on Page 7

Stained Glass Shapes

When baked, these colorful cookies have see-through candy "windows" that look like colored glass. You can use a combination of colors and shapes. Don't restrict yourself to cutting out only one area from the center of the cookie. You can find small cookie cutters (or even a thimble will work) and cut several areas, then fill them with different colors of candy. Try this at Easter time using an egg-shaped cookie and pastel candy colors.

The amount of crushed candy you need will vary somewhat depending on what sizes your cookie cutters are and how many colors you want to use. You can start with a small amount and then crush additional candies as you need them. A little bit goes a long way.

1 recipe Basic Cookie Dough, chilled
$1/4-1/3$ cup crushed hard candies*

Preheat oven to 350°. Divide dough in half, keeping half not used in refrigerator. Roll dough out to $1/8$-inch thickness. Cut shapes with cookie cutter, then cut smaller design out of center, taking care to leave a $1/2$ inch to $3/4$-inch dough border.

Rolled

Place cut-out cookie carefully on cookie sheet covered with foil. Fill cut-out center with crushed candy. The amount needed will vary depending upon the size of the cut-out area. Try to keep the candy in the cut-out area and not get it on the cookie itself or you'll end up coloring the dough.

Bake for 10 to 12 minutes. Remove from oven and let cookies cool completely, then gently remove cookies from foil by peeling the foil away from them.

*Crush the hard candy by putting it in a resealable plastic bag and pounding it gently with a mallet.

Basic Cookie Dough Recipe on Page 7

Anise Cut-Outs

If you like the taste of licorice, you'll like these cookies. They are crispy and light with a hint of licorice.

1 recipe Basic Cookie Dough
1 teaspoon anise seed
1 teaspoon anise extract
1/4 cup sugar
1/2 teaspoon cinnamon

Preheat oven to 350°. In medium bowl, add anise seeds and anise extract to Basic Cookie Dough. Beat until well blended.

In small bowl, combine sugar and cinnamon and mix well.

Roll dough out on lightly floured surface to 1/8-inch thickness. Either cut into squares with sharp knife or cut out shapes with cookie cutter.

Place cookies on lightly greased cookie sheet and sprinkle a little of the cinnamon and sugar mixture over each.

Bake for 10 minutes. Remove from oven and let cookies cool on cookie sheet for 1 minute before transferring to cooling rack. (Makes 3 to 3 1/2 dozen.)

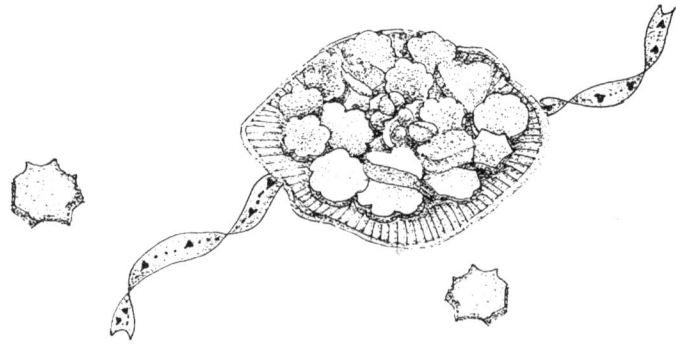

Strawberry Delights

These colorful, pretty cookies are easy to make and look extra special.

1 recipe Basic Cookie Dough, chilled
1 cup strawberry filling (approximately a 12 ounce can)
$1/2$ cup ground almonds

Preheat oven to 375°. Divide Basic Cookie Dough in half and roll out one half at a time, keeping other half refrigerated until ready to use.

Roll dough to $1/4$-inch thickness on a well-floured surface. Cut out cookie circles with 2 inch or $2\ 1/2$-inch diameter biscuit cutter or round cookie cutter.

Place cookies 2 inches apart on ungreased cookie. Spread about $3/4$ teaspoonful of filling in center of each cookie and sprinkle almonds over top. Carefully bring edge of one side of cookie to middle of cookie. Fold the other side in the same way, overlapping the first edge slightly.

Bake for 10 minutes or until edges are lightly browned. Remove from oven and let cookies cool on cookie sheet for 1 minute before transferring to cooling rack. (Makes 3 to $3\ 1/2$ dozen.)

Basic Cookie Dough Recipe on Page 7

Date-Filled Half-Moons

These little puffy crescent-shaped cookies are stuffed with a rich and flavorful filling. Although they'd be great any time of the year, they are especially nice around Thanksgiving and go really well with the other seasonal flavors.

    1 recipe Basic Cookie Dough
    1 tablespoon orange zest (grated orange rind)
    3/4 cup packed brown sugar
    1 tablespoon flour
    Pinch salt
    1/2 cup water
    1/2 cup chopped dates
    1/2 teaspoon cinnamon
    1 cup finely chopped walnuts

Mix Basic Cookie Dough with orange zest until thoroughly blended and chill for several hours or overnight.

Prepare filling. Combine brown sugar, flour, salt, water, dates and cinnamon in medium saucepan and bring to a boil. Cook for 4 minutes, stirring frequently, until mixture is thickened. (While mixture is cooking, try to mash the dates using the back of a spoon or a potato masher.)

Remove from heat and let cool to lukewarm. Stir in nuts.

Preheat oven to 375°. Divide dough in half and work with one half at a time. Roll dough out into a circle 1/8-inch thick. Cut circles using 2 1/2 inch or 3-inch round cookie cutter. Place dough circles 1 inch apart on lightly greased cookie sheet.

Place scant teaspoon of filling on one half of each dough circle, keeping it 1/4 inch from the edge of the dough round. (The amount of filling you use will vary depending on the size of the dough circles you cut. You may need to adjust the filling slightly so you have the right amount for the size of the cookie you're making.)

Gently lift the half of the dough circle without filling and lap it over the half with the filling, keeping edges even. Crimp edges closed using tip of a fork and prick the top of the cookie before baking.

Bake for 8 to 10 minutes, just until edges begin to brown. Remove from oven and let cool for 1 minute, then transfer to cooling rack. (Makes 3 to 3 1/2 dozen.)

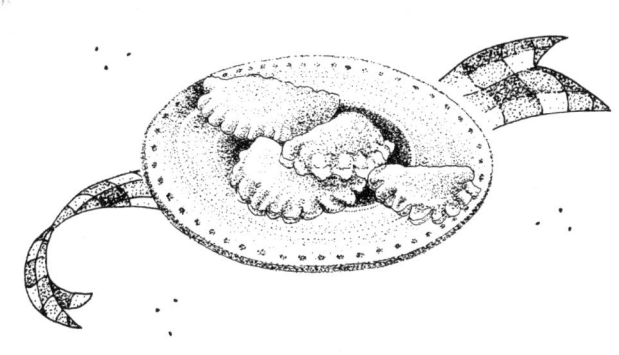

Basic Cookie Dough Recipe on Page 7

Rolled

Cherry "Turnovers"

1 recipe Basic Cookie Dough, chilled
1 cup cherry pie filling, with cherries mashed*
½ cup powdered sugar
¼ teaspoon almond extract
2 teaspoons warm water

Preheat oven to 375°. Divide dough in half, keeping one half refrigerated while you roll the other half into a circle ⅛-inch thick.

Using a 2 ½ inch or 3-inch round cookie cutter, cut circles of dough, placing half the circles on lightly greased cookie sheet.

*To mash the cherries in the pie filling, I put the filling in a small bowl or measuring cup and then use a fork to mash them. The whole cherries are much too large for a small cookie like this.

Place a scant teaspoon of filling on one half of each dough round on the cookie sheet, taking care to keep filling ¼ inch from the border. (You'll need to adjust the amount of filling to the size of the rounds. If you're using a 2 ½-inch cookie cutter, you'll need to use about a half teaspoon of filling.)

Gently lift the side of dough without filling to cover the side with filling, aligning edges of dough. Crimp the edges with a fork to seal them.

Remove from oven and let cookies cool on cookie sheet for 1 minute, then transfer to cooling rack. (Makes 3 to 3 ½ dozen.)

When cool, drizzle with glaze. To make the glaze, combine the powdered sugar, almond extract and water in a small bowl or measuring cup. Mix well.

Use a spoon to scoop up the glaze and then drizzle in a fine stream over the cookies or place the glaze in a small plastic bag, like a sandwich bag. Twist the bag above the glaze and snip the corner. You can get better control this way by using just enough pressure to keep a steady stream of glaze coming out.

Apricot-Filled Treats

These are very similar to the "Mincemeat Pies." Both complement each other wonderfully and look great when served together on a large platter.

♥ ♥ ♥

    2 tablespoons sugar
    1/8 teaspoon cinnamon
    Pinch of ground nutmeg
    1 recipe Basic Cookie Dough, chilled
    1/2–3/4 cup apricot preserves

Preheat oven to 375°. In small bowl, combine the sugar, cinnamon and nutmeg. Stir until well mixed. Set aside.

Roll Basic Cookie Dough to 1/8-inch thickness. Cut out rounds using 2 1/2-inch or 3-inch cookie cutter. Place half the rounds 2 inches apart on lightly greased cookie sheet.

Place a teaspoon of preserves in the center of each round, then place another round on top.

Crimp the edges using the tip of a fork to seal them. Sprinkle a little of the sugar mixture over each cookie and bake for 10 to 12 minutes.

Remove from oven and let cookies cool on cookie sheet for 1 minute, then transfer to cooling rack. (Makes about 2 dozen.)

Basic Cookie Dough Recipe on Page 7

Apple Pie Bites

These fantastic little cookies taste just like apple pie, but can be eaten without a fork. These adorable little bite-sized half-moons filled with apple pie spices and flavor are also much easier to make than an apple pie.

Be sure and serve these soon after they're baked because the filling has a lot of moisture and the cookie absorbs it and can become very soft. It's best to store them in a single layer in a loosely-covered container.

> 1 recipe Basic Cookie Dough, chilled
> $1/2$ teaspoon, plus $1/8$ teaspoon cinnamon
> 2 tablespoons sugar
> 1 cup apple pie filling, with apples finely chopped*

Mix $1/2$ teaspoon cinnamon into Basic Cookie Dough. Chill.

In small bowl, combine sugar and remaining $1/8$ teaspoon cinnamon. Mix well and set aside.

Preheat oven to 375°. Divide dough in half, keeping one half refrigerated while you roll the other half into a circle $1/8$-inch thick.

Using a 2 $1/2$ inch or 3-inch round cookie cutter, cut circles of dough, placing half the circles on lightly greased cookie sheet.

> *To chop the large pieces of apple in the pie filling, I place the filling in a small bowl or measuring cup and then use a sharp knife to slice it into finer pieces. The filling usually comes with apple slices that are too large for a small cookie like this.

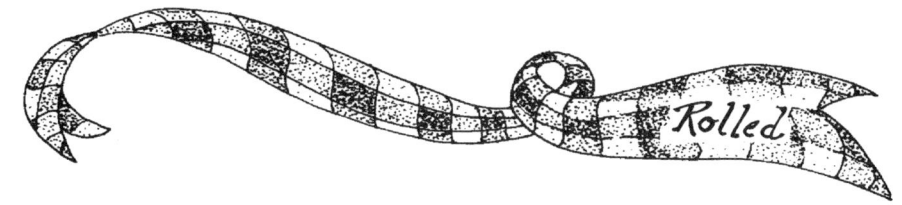

Rolled

Place a scant teaspoon of filling on one half of each dough round on the cookie sheet, taking care to keep filling $1/4$ inch from the border. (You'll need to adjust the amount of filling you use to the size of the rounds you're using. If you're using a $2\ 1/2$-inch cookie cutter, you'll need to use about a half teaspoon of filling.)

Gently lift the side of dough without filling to cover the side with filling, aligning edges of dough. Crimp the edges with a fork to seal them.

Sprinkle each cookie with a little of the sugar and cinnamon mixture, then bake for 8 to 10 minutes, until edges are lightly brown.

Remove from oven and let cookies cool on cookie sheet for 1 minute, then transfer to cooling rack. (Makes 3 to $3\ 1/2$ dozen.)

Basic Cookie Dough Recipe on Page 7

Rugalach

This cookie version of a bakery favorite combines the flavor of nuts, jam and cinnamon into a tasty little treat that tastes a lot like the real thing. They're easy to make and full of flavor. You can vary the flavor by choosing different flavor preserves. I frequently make half the batch with raspberry and half with apricot for a little variety.

♥ ♥ ♥

1 tablespoon sugar
1/4 teaspoon cinnamon
1 recipe Basic Cookie Dough, chilled
3/4 cup raspberry, blackberry or cherry preserves
1/2 cup ground pecans or walnuts
1/2 cup raisins
1 egg, slightly beaten

Preheat oven to 375°. Combine sugar and cinnamon in small bowl and mix well. Set aside.

Divide dough in half and roll out one half at a time, keeping other half refrigerated until ready to use. Roll dough out on well-floured surface into circle about 1/4-inch thick.

Spread half the preserves evenly over the surface. Sprinkle half the nuts evenly over preserves. Sprinkle half the raisins evenly on top.

Using sharp knife, cut circle into 16 wedges. Starting at the wide end of each wedge, carefully roll the dough. (You'll end up with a crescent shape.)

Place 3 inches apart on lightly greased cookie sheet. Using pastry brush, brush egg lightly over surface, then sprinkle a little of the cinnamon-sugar mixture over each. Repeat with remaining half of Basic Cookie Dough and ingredients.

Bake for 15 to 18 minutes, until edges are nicely browned. Remove from oven and immediately transfer cookies to cooling rack. (Makes about 3 1/2 dozen.)

Mincemeat "Pies"

These are cute little things! Essentially little bite size pies, these round, pillow-shaped treats are a lot easier to serve and eat. The egg-wash brushed over them before they are baked gives them a nice shiny finish.

1 recipe Basic Cookie Dough, chilled
1/3 cup mincemeat filling*
1 egg, slightly beaten

Preheat oven to 375°. Divide chilled Basic Cookie Dough in half and keep one half in the refrigerator while you roll the other half out to 1/8-inch thickness.

Using a 2 1/2 inch or 3-inch round cookie cutter, cut circles of dough and place half of them 2 inches apart on lightly greased cookie sheets.

Place a teaspoon of mincemeat filling in the center of each dough round on the cookie sheet, and then place another dough round on top. Crimp the edges of the cookies by using the tip of a fork to press the seams together.

Then, with a pastry brush, put a thin layer of egg over each cookie. Bake for 8 to 10 minutes, until edges are lightly browned.

Remove from oven and let cookies cool on cookie sheet for 1 minute before transferring to cooling rack.
(Makes about 2 dozen.)

*Use any mincemeat pie filling from a jar or can.

Basic Cookie Dough Recipe on Page 7

Pecan Whirls

This is a fast little cookie, but one that looks like you spent a lot of time making it. If you make your dough ahead of time, you simply open a can of filling, make the cookies, chill, then slice and bake.

1 recipe Basic Cookie Dough, chilled
1 cup pecan filling*

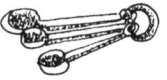

Divide Basic Cookie Dough in half, keeping one half refrigerated while you roll out the other half into a 9 x 13-inch rectangle.

Carefully spread the pecan filling evenly over the dough, extending it to within $1/4$ inch of the edges on the short ends.

Starting with short end, roll dough jellyroll fashion. Wrap in plastic wrap or wax paper (taking care to keep dough roll from bending) and chill for several hours. Repeat with other half of Basic Cookie Dough.

Preheat oven to 375°. Unwrap each roll of dough and slice into pieces $1/4$-inch thick. Place pieces flat side down and 2 inches apart on lightly greased cookie sheet.

Bake for 8 to 10 minutes or until edges begin to brown. Remove from oven and let cookies cool on cookie sheet for 1 minute, then transfer to cooling rack. (Makes about 4 dozen.)

*Pecan filling comes in a can.

Pineapple Pinwheels

1 recipe Basic Cookie Dough
$1/4$ cup shortening
1 tablespoon lemon zest (grated lemon rind)
$1/2$ cup pineapple preserves, divided
$1/2$ cup ground or finely chopped nuts, divided

In medium bowl, combine Basic Cookie Dough with shortening and lemon zest. Beat until dough is well-blended.

Divide dough in half. On lightly floured surface, roll out one half into a rectangle about 9 x13 inches in diameter. Spread $1/4$ cup pineapple preserves evenly over dough. Sprinkle $1/4$ cup of nuts evenly over preserves.

Starting with short end, roll dough jellyroll fashion. Repeat with other half of dough.

Wrap each dough roll in plastic and refrigerate for several hours.

Preheat oven to 375°. Slice each roll into pieces $1/4$-inch thick and place 2 inches apart on well greased cookie sheet. Bake for 10 minutes, or until edges are brown.

Remove from oven and let cookies cool on cookie sheet for 1 minute, then transfer to cooling rack. (Makes 3 $1/2$ to 4 dozen.)

I find it's easiest to roll the dough between two sheets of wax paper. Not only is it less messy but it also ensures the dough doesn't stick to the rolling pin. When I'm ready to wrap dough roll, I simply use the wax paper it's sitting on.

Basic Cookie Dough Recipe on Page 7

Chocolate Spirals

1 recipe Basic Cookie Dough
2 (1 ounce) squares unsweetened chocolate, melted, cooled slightly

Divide Basic Cookie Dough in half. Place one half in medium-size bowl and add melted chocolate. Beat until chocolate is completely mixed into dough.

Roll out remaining plain half of dough into a rectangle about 8-inches wide and 12-inches long. Roll out chocolate dough to the same dimensions.

Place chocolate dough on top of plain dough and starting with the longest side, roll jellyroll fashion into a log. Wrap dough carefully and chill for an hour or so.

Preheat oven to 375°. Remove wrapping from dough, and with sharp knife, slice into $1/4$-inch pieces. Place cookie slices 2 inches apart on ungreased cookie sheet.

Bake for about 10 minutes, then remove from oven and let cookies cool on cookie sheet for 1 minute. Transfer to cooling rack. (Makes 2 to 2 $1/2$ dozen.)

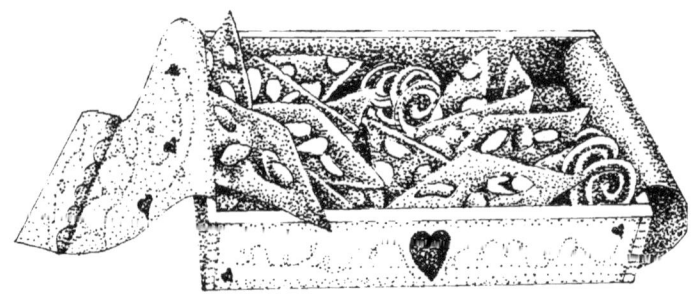

Almond Cherry Pinwheels

This is another one of those recipes I like so much because of the speed with which you can make a snack that looks and tastes fantastic. I like to prepare the dough ahead of time so I can slice and bake them when I'm in the mood for a fresh batch. The spiral shape is intriguing and looks difficult, but is really very easy to do.

1 recipe Basic Cookie Dough
1/4 cup shortening
1/2 teaspoon almond extract
1/2 cup cherry preserves, divided
1/2 cup ground or finely chopped almonds, divided

In medium bowl, combine Basic Cookie Dough with shortening and almond extract. Beat until dough is well-blended.

Divide dough in half. On lightly floured surface, roll out one half into a 9 x 13-inch rectangle. Spread 1/4 cup cherry preserves evenly over dough. Sprinkle 1/4 cup almonds evenly over preserves.

Starting with short end, roll dough jellyroll fashion.

Repeat with other half of dough.

Wrap each dough roll in plastic and refrigerate for several hours.

Preheat oven to 375°. Slice each roll into pieces 1/4-inch thick and place 2 inches apart on well greased cookie sheet. Bake for 10 minutes or until edges are brown.

Remove from oven and let cookies cool on pan for 1 minute, then transfer to cooling rack. (Makes 3 1/2 to 4 dozen.)

Basic Cookie Dough Recipe on Page 7

Date Nut Pinwheels

1 cup finely chopped dates
½ cup sugar
½ cup water
1 recipe Basic Cookie Dough, chilled
½ cup ground walnuts

In small saucepan, combine dates, sugar and water. Bring to a simmer and cook, stirring occasionally, over medium heat for 3 to 4 minutes, until mixture is thickened. Remove from heat and let cool to room temperature.

Divide Basic Cookie Dough in half. Roll out one half into a rectangle ¼-inch thick. Spread half date mixture evenly over dough, bringing it to within ½ inch of the edge of dough. Sprinkle half the walnuts evenly over date mixture.

Starting with long side, roll dough jellyroll fashion. Wrap in plastic wrap and chill for a couple of hours. Repeat with other half of dough.

Preheat oven to 375°. Slice dough rolls into ¼-inch pieces and place 2 inches apart on lightly greased cookie sheet. Bake for 10 to 12 minutes or until lightly browned. Remove from oven and let cookies cool on cookie sheet for 1 minute before transferring to cooling rack. (Makes 3 ½ to 4 dozen.)

Ginger Jam Sandwich Cookies

1 recipe Basic Cookie Dough
2 teaspoons ground ginger
1/2 teaspoon cinnamon
1/4 teaspoon ground cloves
1/2 cup strawberry jam

Preheat oven to 350°. In medium bowl, combine ginger, cinnamon and cloves with Basic Cookie Dough, and mix well.

Roll small pieces of dough into balls about 3/4 inch to 1 inch in diameter. Place 2 inches apart on ungreased cookie sheet. Flatten slightly with bottom of glass dipped in sugar.

Bake for 10 to 12 minutes or until lightly browned around edges.

Remove from oven and let cookies cool on cookie sheet for 1 minute before transferring to cooling rack.

When completely cool, place 1/2 teaspoonful of jam into center back of one cookie and top with flat side of another cookie. Press lightly to distribute jam to edges.

If you want, take a little powdered sugar and sift it over the cookies. It makes a great finishing touch. (Makes 2 1/2 to 3 dozen.)

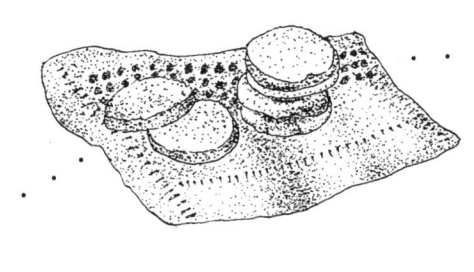

Basic Cookie Dough Recipe on Page 7

Lemon Raisin Sandwich Cookies

If you prefer the flavor of dates, you can replace the raisins in this recipe with them, chopped of course. They'll taste just as good with the citrus flavor of the cookie.

    1 recipe Basic Cookie Dough
    1 tablespoon lemon juice
    1 tablespoon lemon zest (grated lemon rind)
    $2/3$ cup raisins
    3 tablespoons sugar

Preheat oven to 400°. In medium bowl, combine Basic Cookie Dough with lemon juice and lemon zest. Beat well. Stir in raisins.

Form dough into balls 1 1/2-inches wide. Roll balls in sugar to coat and place 2 inches apart on ungreased cookie sheet. Flatten each with the slightly greased bottom of a glass.

Bake for 8 to 10 minutes, until edges are just lightly browned. Remove from oven and let cookies cool on cookie sheet for 1 minute, then transfer to cooling rack.

When cool, spread flat side of one cookie with generous amount of filling. Place another cookie over filling, flat side down and press together lightly. (Makes 1 1/2 dozen finished cookies.)

When I make sandwich cookies, I like to give them neat little edges by running the tip of a butter knife between the two cookies after I fill them, turning the cookie as I go, to smooth the filling and even it out.

Filling

1 (8 ounce) package cream cheese, softened
½ cup butter or margarine, softened
½ teaspoon vanilla
4 cups powdered sugar

In small mixing bowl, beat cream cheese and butter until light and fluffy. Beat in vanilla and then powdered sugar a little at a time, beating well after each addition.

Basic Cookie Dough Recipe on Page 7

Jam-Filled Sandwich Cookies

1 recipe Basic Cookie Dough, chilled
1/3-1/2 cup jam or jelly
Powdered sugar for garnish

Preheat oven to 375°. Divide Basic Cookie Dough in half and work with one half at a time, keeping other half refrigerated until ready to use.

Roll cookie dough out into a circle 1/8-inch thick. Cut desired shapes with cookie cutter. Take very small cutter and cut a center out of half the cookies. Place cookies 2 inches apart on ungreased cookie sheet.

Bake for 8 to 10 minutes or until cookies are lightly browned around edges.

Remove from oven and let cookies cool on cookie sheet for 1 minute, then transfer to cooling rack.

When cool, place a half teaspoonful of jam on the center back of one solid cookie and spread jam almost to edges. Place a cookie with a cut out center over the jam and press lightly to seal.

Just before serving, dust a little powdered sugar over cookies.

Chocolate Peanut Butter Sandwich Cookies

1 recipe Basic Cookie Dough
2 squares unsweetened chocolate, melted
3 tablespoons sugar

Preheat oven to 350°. In medium bowl add melted chocolate to Basic Cookie Dough and blend well.

Shape dough into 1 1/2-inch balls and place 3 inches apart on ungreased cookie sheet. Use bottom of a glass greased and dipped in sugar to flatten each cookie.

Bake for 10 minutes, then remove from oven. Let cookies cool on cookie sheet for 1 minute before transferring to cooling rack.

When cool, frost flat side of one cookie with about 1 teaspoon of Peanut Butter Filling, and then place flat side of another cookie on top. Press together lightly.

Peanut Butter Filling

1/4 cup creamy peanut butter
1 1/2 cups powdered sugar
2-3 tablespoons milk
1/2 teaspoon vanilla

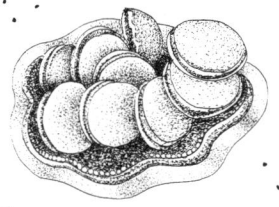

Combine peanut butter, powdered sugar, milk and vanilla in a medium bowl. Beat on medium speed with hand mixer until mixture is smooth and creamy.

Basic Cookie Dough Recipe on Page 7

German Chocolate Sandwich Cookies

1 recipe Basic Cookie Dough
1/4 cup shortening
1/2 cup packed brown sugar
2/3 cup cocoa powder
2 tablespoons milk

Preheat oven to 350°. In large bowl, combine Basic Cookie Dough with shortening, brown sugar, cocoa powder and milk. Beat until thoroughly blended and dough is evenly colored.

Roll pieces of dough into balls 1 1/2-inches wide and place 3 inches apart on ungreased cookie sheet. Take the bottom of a glass (greased with a little shortening or butter) and flatten each dough ball.

Bake for 10 minutes, remove from oven, and let cool cookies cool on cookie sheet for 1 minute. Transfer to cooling rack.

When cool, place about 1 teaspoonful of filling on the back half (flat side) of one cookie, place another cookie (flat side down) on top and press together firmly. (Try to get the filling to the edges of the cookie.) Makes 2 dozen finished cookies.

Warm from the Oven

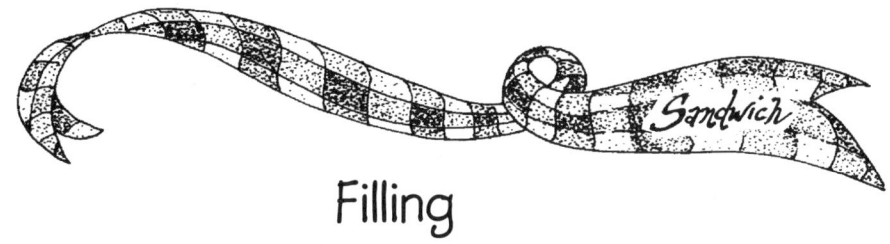

Filling

- ½ cup butter or margarine
- ½ cup packed brown sugar
- ¼ cup light corn syrup
- 1 teaspoon vanilla
- 1 cup flaked coconut
- 1 cup finely chopped pecans

Melt butter in a medium saucepan over medium heat. Stir in brown sugar and corn syrup. Bring to a simmer, stirring constantly, and cook for about 3 to 4 minutes, until mixture is thickened.

Remove from heat and stir in vanilla, then coconut and pecans. Use while warm.

Basic Cookie Dough Recipe on Page 7

Spicy Molasses Sandwich Cookies

1 recipe Basic Cookie Dough
1/2 cup shortening
1/2 cup molasses
1/2 teaspoon cinnamon
1/4 teaspoon ground nutmeg
1/4 teaspoon ginger
1/4 teaspoon ground cloves
1/2 cup quick-cooking oats

Preheat oven to 375°. In large bowl, combine Basic Cookie Dough with shortening, molasses, cinnamon, nutmeg, ginger and cloves. Beat until well mixed. Blend in oats.

Drop by rounded teaspoonful onto ungreased cookie sheet. Bake for 10 minutes. Remove from oven and let cookies cool on cookie sheet 1 minute, then transfer to cooling rack.

When cool, place a teaspoonful of filling on the back side (flat side) of one cookie, then top with flat side of another. Press lightly to force filling to edges of cookie.

Filling

3/4 cup butter or margarine
2 cups powdered sugar
1/8 teaspoon salt
1 teaspoon vanilla
1 tablespoon milk
1 (7 ounce) jar marshmallow creme

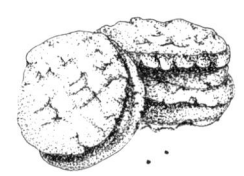

In medium bowl, cream butter, sugar, salt, vanilla and milk. Add marshmallow creme and beat with hand mixer until mixture is smooth.

Spicy Crumb Cake

1 recipe Basic Cookie Dough
1 teaspoon cinnamon
1 teaspoon ground nutmeg
1/4 teaspoon allspice
1/4 teaspoon ground cloves
1 cup buttermilk

1/2 cup flour
1/2 cup plus 2 tablespoons sugar
2 tablespoons butter or margarine, softened

Preheat oven to 350°. In large bowl, combine Basic Cookie Dough with cinnamon, nutmeg, allspice, cloves and buttermilk. Beat on medium speed to blend, stopping to scrape bowl as necessary.

Pour batter into greased 9 x 9-inch baking pan.

In small bowl, combine flour and sugar. Cut in butter until mixture is crumbly. Sprinkle over batter in pan.

Bake for 50 minutes to 1 hour or until crumb topping is nicely browned and cake tester comes out clean. Cool and cut into squares.

Basic Cookie Dough Recipe on Page 7

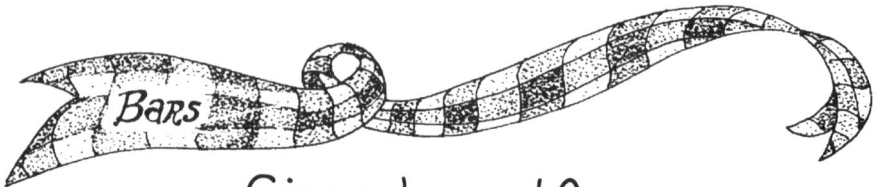

Bars

Gingerbread Squares with Brown Sugar Frosting

Would you believe you can also use the Basic Cookie Dough recipe to create a cake? This easy gingerbread is a modified version of a recipe given to me by my friend, Michele. It's loaded with flavor and as moist as can be. It's great even without the frosting! A little powdered sugar dusted over the cooled cake does the trick.

    1 recipe Basic Cookie Dough
    1/2 cup molasses
    2 teaspoons ginger
    2 teaspoons cinnamon
    1/2 teaspoon ground cloves
    3/4 cup hot black coffee

Preheat oven to 350°. In large bowl, combine Basic Cookie Dough with molasses, ginger, cinnamon and cloves. Beat on low speed, adding coffee a little at a time until the mixture is thoroughly blended.

Pour batter into greased and floured 9-inch square pan.

Bake for 40 minutes or until cake tester comes out clean. Let cool and then frost with Brown Sugar Frosting.

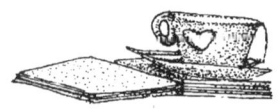

Brown Sugar Frosting

2 tablespoons butter or margarine
2 tablespoons evaporated milk
1/4 cup packed brown sugar
Pinch salt
1/2 teaspoon vanilla
1 cup powdered sugar

In small saucepan, combine butter, evaporated milk, brown sugar and salt. Cook and stir over low heat until sugar is dissolved.

Remove from heat and let cool. Stir in vanilla, then beat in powdered sugar until frosting consistency is reached.

Basic Cookie Dough Recipe on Page 7

Chocolate Covered Banana Bars

These yummy banana-flavored bars are moist and easy to make! Just add four ingredients to the Basic Cookie Dough to create. Frosting is almost automatic!

- 1 recipe Basic Cookie Dough
- 1/3 cup packed brown sugar
- 1 cup mashed ripe bananas (about 2 large)
- 1/2 cup sour cream
- 2 cups milk chocolate or semi-sweet chocolate chips, divided

Preheat oven to 350°. In large bowl, combine Basic Cookie Dough with brown sugar, bananas and sour cream. Beat on medium high speed until mixture is smooth. Stir in 1 cup chocolate chips.

Spread batter in greased and floured 9 x 13-inch baking pan. Bake for 25 to 30 minutes or until cake tester comes out clean.

Immediately upon removing from oven, sprinkle remaining cup of chocolate chips evenly over surface and let them sit for 5 minutes. Spread softened chips over surface to frost. When cool, cut into bars and serve.

Index

Almond Cherry Pinwheels 75
Anise Cut-Outs 62
Apple Cranberry Cookies 24
Apple Pie Bites 68
Applesauce Drops 16
Apricot-Filled Treats 67
Banana Cookies with Banana Frosting 19
Bars
    Brown Sugar Frosting 87
    Chocolate Covered Banana Bars 88
    Gingerbread Squares with Brown Sugar Frosting 86
    Spicy Crumb Cake 85
Basic Cookie Dough 7
Brandied Fruitcake Cookies 9
Brandy-Dipped Apricot Delights 17
Brown Sugar Frosting 87
Cherry Caps 57
Cherry Turnovers 66
Chocolate Almond Fingers 40
Chocolate Chip Hazelnut Mounds 58
Chocolate

    Chocolate-Topped Brownie Bites 8
    Chocolate Almond Fingers 40
    Chocolate Covered Cherry Delights 34
    Chocolate Fudge Thumbprints 36
    Chocolate Glaze 8
Chocolate Thumbprints 41
Chocolate Macadamia Nut Cookies 30
Chocolate Striped Cookies 44
Chocolate Mint Thins 48
Chocolate-Covered Mocha Balls 53
Chocolate Coating 55
Chocolate Chip Hazelnut Mounds 58
Chocolate Spirals 74
Chocolate Peanut Butter Sandwich Cookies 81
Chocolate Covered Banana Bars 88
Fudge Filling 37
Mocha Chip Drops 12
Orange Mocha Drops 27
Peanut Butter and Chocolate Kisses 38
Renna's Cappuccino Drops 33
Traditional Chocolate Chip Cookies 31
White Chocolate Cherry Rounds 14
Chocolate Coating 55
Chocolate Covered Banana Bars 88
Chocolate Covered Cherry Delights 34
Chocolate Dipped Malted Milk Rounds 54
Chocolate Fudge Thumbprints 36

Index

Chocolate Glaze 40
Chocolate Mint Thins 48
Chocolate Peanut Butter Sandwich Cookies 81
Chocolate Spirals 74
Chocolate Striped Cookies 44
Chocolate Thumbprints 41
Chocolate-Covered Mocha Balls 53
Chocolate-Topped Brownie Bites 8
Crispy Pecan Thins 21
Date Nut Pinwheels 76
Date-Filled Half-Moons 64
Date-Studded Orange Cookies 20
Drop
Apple Cranberry Cookies 24
Applesauce Drops 16
Banana Cookies with Banana Frosting 19
    Brandied Fruitcake Cookies 9
    Brandy-Dipped Apricot Delights 17
    Chocolate-Topped Brownie Bites 8
Crispy Pecan Thins 21
Date-Studded Orange Cookies 20
Hearty Carrot Cookies 18
    Hearty Trail Mix Cookies 23
    Lemon Zucchini Cookies 26
    Maple Iced Walnut Drops 11
    Mocha Chip Drops 12
    Oatmeal Raisin Cookies 22
    Orange Glaze 29
    Orange Glazed Fruitcake Rounds 28
    Orange Mocha Drops 27
    Pfefferneusse 15
    Ranger Cookies 25
    Spicy Iced Pumpkin Drops 13
    Spicy Pineapple Cookies 10
    Traditional Chocolate Chip Cookies 31
    White Chocolate Cherry Rounds 14
    White Chocolate Macadamia Nut Cookies 30
    Festive Cranberry Cookies 42
    Fudge Filling 37
German Chocolate Sandwich Cookies 82
Ginger Jam Sandwich Cookies 77
Gingerbread Squares with Brown Sugar Frosting 86
Hearty Carrot Cookies 18
Hearty Trail Mix Cookies 23
Heavenly Holiday Rounds 47
Fruits
Almond Cherry Pinwheels 75

Index

Apple Cranberry Cookies 24
Apple Pie Bites 68
Applesauce Drops 16
Apricot-Filled Treats 67
Banana Cookies with banana Frosting 19
Brandied Fruitcake Cookies 9
Brandy-Dipped Apricot Delights 17
Cherry "Turnovers" 66
Cherry Caps 57
Chocolate Covered Banana Bars 88
Chocolate Covered Cherry Delights 34
Chocolate Thumbprints 41
Chocolate-Topped Brownie Bites 8
Date-filled Half-Moons 64
Date-Studded Orange Cookies 20
    Festive Cranberry Cookies 42
    Ginger Jam Sandwich Cookies 77
    Hearty Carrot Cookies 18
    Hearty Trail Mix Cookies 23
    Heavenly Holiday Rounds 47
    Jam–Filled Sandwich Cookies 80
    Lemon Raisin Sandwich Cookies 78
    Mincemeat "Pies" 71
    Nutty Lemon Rounds 56
    Oatmeal Raisin Cookies 22
    Orange Glaze 29
    Orange Glazed Fruitcake Rounds 28
    Orange Mocha Drops 27
    Orange Slices 49
    Pineapple Pinwheels 73
    Raisin Gingersnaps 52
Rugalach 70
Spiced Iced Pumpkin Drops 13
Spicy Pineapple Cookies 10
Strawberry Delights 63
Tropical Thumbprint Cookies 39
White Chocolate Cherry Rounds 14
Jam-Filled Sandwich Cookies 80
Lemon Anise Rounds 50
Lemon Raisin Sandwich Cookies 78
Lemon Zucchini Cookies 26
Maple Iced Walnut Drops 11
Mincemeat Pies 71
Mocha Chip Drops 12
Molasses Rounds 59
Nutty Lemon Rounds 56
Oatmeal Raisin Cookies 22
Orange Glaze 29

Index

Orange Glazed Fruitcake Rounds 28
Orange Mocha Drops 27
Orange Slices 49
Peanut Butter and Chocolate Kisses 38
Peanut Butter and Jelly Thumbprints 32
Peanut Butter Filling 81
Pecan Whirls 72
Peppermint Candy Cane Cookies 43
Pfefferneusse 15
Pineapple Pinwheels 73

Icings & Glazes
    Banana Frosting 19
    Brandy Icing 17
    Brown Sugar Frosting 87
    Chocolate Coating 48
    Chocolate Glaze 40
    Chocolate Glaze 8
    Fudge Filling 37
    German Chocoate Filling 83
    Lemon Raisin Filling 79
    Maple Icing 11
    Orange Frosting 13
    Orange Glaze 29
    Orange Icing 27
    Peanut Butter Filling 81
    Spicy Molasses Sandwich Cookies Filling 84

Jams & Jellies
Almond Cherry Pinwheels 75
Apricot-Filled Treats 67
Chocolate Thumbprints 41
Ginger Jam Sandwich Cookies 77
Jam-Filled Sandwich Cookies 80
Peanut Butter and Jelly Thumbprints 32
Pineapple pinwheels 73
Rugalach 70
Strawberry Delights 63
Tropical Thumbprint Cookies 39

Nuts
Almond Cherry Pinwheels 75
Apple Cranberry Cookies 24
Banana Cookies with Banana Frosting 19
Brandied Fruitcake Cookies 9
Chocolate Almond Fingers 40
Chocolate Chip Hazelnut Mounds 58
Chocolate-Topped brownie Bites 8
Chocolate Striped Cookies 44
Crispy Pecan Thins 21

Index

Date Nut Pinwheels 76
Date-Filled Half-Moons 64
Festive Cranberry Cookies 42
German Chocolate Sandwich Cookies/Filling 83
Hearty Carrot Cookies 18
Lemon Zucchini Cookies 26
Maple Iced Walnut Drops 11
Nutty Lemon Rounds 56
Orange Slices 49
Pecan Whirls 72
Pineapple Pinwheels 73
Rugalach 70
Spicy Iced Pumpkin Drops 13
Traditional Chocolate Chip Cookies 31
White Chocolate Macadamia Nut Cookies 30

Pinwheels
Almond Cherry Pinwheels 75
Chocolate Spirals 74
Date Nut Pinwheels 76
Pecan Whirls 72

Pineapple Pinwheels 73
Raisin Gingersnaps 52
Ranger Cookies 25
Renna's Cappuccino Drops 33

Rolled
Anise Cut-Outs 62
Apple Pie Bites 68
Apricot-Filled Treats 67
Cherry Turnovers 66
Date-Filled Half-Moons 64
Mincemeat Pies 71
Rugalach 70
Stained Glass Shapes 60
Strawberry Delights 63
Rugalach 70

Sandwich
Chocolate Peanut Butter Sandwich Cookies 81
German Chocolate Sandwich Cookies 82
Ginger Jam Sandwich Cookies 77
Jam-Filled Sandwich Cookies 80
Lemon Raisin Sandwich Cookies 78
Peanut Butter Filling 81
Spicy Molasses Sandwich Cookies 84

Shaped
Cherry Caps 57
Chocolate Almond Fingers 40
Chocolate Chip Hazelnut Mounds 58
Chocolate Coating 55

Index

Chocolate Covered Cherry Delights 34
Chocolate Dipped Malted Milk Rounds 54
Chocolate Fudge Thumbprints 36
Chocolate Glaze 40
Chocolate Mint Thins 48
Chocolate Striped Cookies 44
Chocolate Thumbprints 41
Chocolate-Covered Mocha Balls 53
Festive Cranberry Cookies 42
Fudge Filling 37
Heavenly Holiday Rounds 47
Lemon Anise Rounds 50
Molasses Rounds 59
Nutty Lemon Rounds 56
Orange Slices 49
Peanut Butter and Chocolate Kisses 38
Peanut Butter and Jelly Thumbprints 32
Peppermint Candy Cane Cookies 43
Raisin Gingersnaps 52
Renna's Cappuccino Drops 33

Snappy Peanut Butter Cookies 51
Spicy Cinnamon Sugar Twists 46
Tropical Thumbprint Cookies 39
Snappy Peanut Butter Cookies 51
Spicy Cinnamon Sugar Twists 46
Spicy Crumb Cake 85
Spicy Iced Pumpkin Drops 13
Spicy Molasses Sandwich Cookies 84
Spicy Pineapple Cookies 10
Stained Glass Shapes 60
Strawberry Delights 63
Traditional Chocolate Chip Cookies 31
Tropical Thumbprint Cookies 39
White Chocolate Cherry Rounds 14
White Chocolate Macadamia Nut Cookies 30
Vegetables
Hearty Carrot Cookies 18
Lemon Zucchini Cookies 26

cookbook resources® LLC

Cooking With 5 Ingredients
The New Cooking With 4 Ingredients
The Best of Cooking With 3 Ingredients
Gourmet Cooking With 5 Ingredients
Low-Fat Cooking with 4 Ingredients
Quick Fixes With Mixes
Kitchen Keepsakes & More Kitchen Keepsakes
Mother's Recipes
Recipe Keepsakes
Cookie Dough Secrets
Cookbook 25 Years
Best of Busy People's Cookbooks
Pass The Plate
Texas Longhorn Cookbook
Simply Simpatico
Mealtimes and Memories
Holiday Treats
Homecoming
Cookin' With Will Rogers
Best of Lone Star Legacy Cookbook
Little Taste of Texas
Little Taste of Texas II
Southwest Sizzler
Southwest Ole
Class Favorites
Leaving Home

www.cookbookresources.com

To Order Cookie Dough Secrets:

Please send_____ hard copies @ $14.95 (U.S.) each $_____
Please send_____ paperbacks @ $9.95 (U.S.) each $_____
Plus postage/handling @ $4.00 each $_____
Texas residents add sales tax @ $1.08 each $_____
Check or Credit Card (Canada-credit card only) **Total** $_____

Charge to my ☐ VISA or ☐ MasterCard

Account #_____

Expiration Date_____

Signature_____

Mail or Call:
Cookbook Resources
541 Doubletree Drive
Highland Village, TX 75077
Toll-free: 866/229-2665
www.cookbookresources.com

Name_____

Address_____

City_____ State_____ Zip_____

Phone (day)_____ (night)_____

- -

To Order Cookie Dough Secrets:

Please send_____ hard copies @ $14.95 (U.S.) each $_____
Please send_____ paperbacks @ $9.95 (U.S.) each $_____
Plus postage/handling @ $4.00 each $_____
Texas residents add sales tax @ $1.08 each $_____
Check or Credit Card (Canada-credit card only) **Total** $_____

Charge to my ☐ VISA or ☐ MasterCard

Account #_____

Expiration Date_____

Signature_____

Mail or Call:
Cookbook Resources
541 Doubletree Drive
Highland Village, TX 75077
Toll-free: 866/229-2665
www.cookbookresources.com

Name_____

Address_____

City_____ State_____ Zip_____

Phone (day)_____ (night)_____